Order this book online at www.trafford.com/07-2559
or email orders@trafford.com

Most Trafford titles are also available at major online book retailers.

Note for Librarians: A cataloguing record for this book is available from Library
and Archives Canada at www.collectionscanada.ca/amicus/index-e.html

Printed in Victoria, BC, Canada.

ISBN: 978-1-4251-5698-5

*We at Trafford believe that it is the responsibility of us all, as both individuals
and corporations, to make choices that are environmentally and socially sound.
You, in turn, are supporting this responsible conduct each time you purchase a
Trafford book, or make use of our publishing services. To find out how you are
helping, please visit www.trafford.com/responsiblepublishing.html*

*Our mission is to efficiently provide the world's finest, most comprehensive
book publishing service, enabling every author to experience success.
To find out how to publish your book, your way, and have it available
worldwide, visit us online at www.trafford.com/10510*

www.trafford.com

North America & international
toll-free: 1 888 232 4444 (USA & Canada)
phone: 250 383 6864 ♦ fax: 250 383 6804
email: info@trafford.com

The United Kingdom & Europe
phone: +44 (0)1865 487 395 ♦ local rate: 0845 230 9601
facsimile: +44 (0)1865 481 507 ♦ email: info.uk@trafford.com

10 9 8 7 6 5 4 3 2

A Note from the Author
to all those who purchased his first book
The Road Across the Bridge.

I hope you thoroughly enjoyed the read and I hope you were able to get to grips with most of the lessons and had a smile at some of the articles between the main chapters. I did say the card game called Bridge was not an easy game to learn.

Now a Note from the Author
for those who have not acquired his first book
The Road Across the Bridge.

If you have not played Bridge before, you would do well to purchase my previous book because it is specifically aimed at the newcomer to learn the basics of the fascinating card game called Bridge. It will take you slowly through the learning stages at 'ground level' giving you enough detail of the game to enable you to play at your local Bridge club. Many readers commented on the 'easy read' and a book they were able to 'pick up and put down'. This second volume is directed more at the person who already plays Bridge but feels a refresher would improve their game.

Finally, a Note from the Author
addressed to his Brother John

Isn't it about time you stopped spending valuable time knocking that silly little ball round the golf course and did something sensible in your life like learning to play Bridge?

Talking about learning to play Bridge.
Congratulations go to my friends Maureen, Tina, Patrick, Marlene and Bob who persevered over many weeks with my Bridge lessons and who have now enjoyed playing at the local Bridge club. I wish them well with their Bridge and I look forward to partnering them.

Index

Index for Selected Subjects.

Retracing Steps Across the Bridge
By Bryan Stephens

Just Before the Start.

"How much longer are you going to wear those trousers?"

I have written this book not only for those who have read my first book *The Road Across the Bridge* and who now need to run through the basics of the card game called Bridge again but also for those folk who already play Bridge but consider a refresher would improve their game.

What has really prompted me to put pen to paper again so to speak are the number of people I come across who know how to play Bridge in a basic fashion but have little or no idea about some of the intricacies of the game which, to me, make the game so interesting. Like telling their partner on their rebid whether they have a strong or weak opening hand, or discarding a card to show the suit they would like led or asking their partner to bid and at what level following their Double. Things like that.

Playing bridge for some time now, however long that is, I have reached what I consider a reasonable standard which is considerably lower than the standard of some players I know. Never having competed in a major competition, I play at home and at the homes of my friends and at four local Bridge clubs.

Bridge for me is a form of relaxation and I certainly would not be relaxed at a serious Bridge competition. I play regularly at my local clubs and I play to win but am never perturbed if things do not go quite as planned. I am generally happy with the results I achieve. I say generally because there are occasions when I have either made blunders or been just unlucky and have ended up below half way on the results sheet and sometimes bottom. There are times when I 'kick' myself for being so stupid with my play but overall I thoroughly enjoy this wonderful game. Take the other day. Half way through the Club session I opened 1nt and my partner bid and I ended up playing a 2h contract. We do what is called Transfers which I will explain a little latter. Near the end of the game, I claimed the final three tricks and was politely told by my right hand opposition that they were not winners at all only to realize that I had been playing a 1nt contract instead of a contract in 2h which I had bid. Is that short term memory loss or what?

Moving to the English Sussex Coast and meeting neighbours who wanted to learn to play Bridge and also meeting folk whose game was somewhat 'prehistoric', set me about writing a relaxed tutorial on the basics of Bridge in a down to earth fashion. My earlier book *The Road Across the Bridge* sets out not only a description of the playing cards but also of trumps, minibridge and then on to Bridge itself where the bidding is described and some aspect of the play. Between each of the tutorial chapters are what I have called Betwixt Chapters which tell of happenings of what one would expect at the local Bridge club, incidences at my home and observations of life in general not necessarily anything at all to do with Bridge.

There are dozens and dozens of worthy Bridge tutorials on the market but the ones I came across when I was learning to play, in my opinion, fell short of what was required by those needing to learn the basics of the game and who, like myself, often need to read an instruction several times before it properly 'sinks in'.

I never profess to be an expert at anything, including Bridge – far from it. I'm most definitely Mr Average and my relaxed first tutorial was aimed at giving those wishing to learn Bridge as much knowledge as I had gained over the years which I must admit is somewhat limited compared with the knowledge of most, if not all, authors on the subject. Take on board the knowledge I have gained and you will have a fair grounding in the best game of cards I have ever played. Those who wish to develop to greater skills should read some of the many books written by the experts.

There are various ways to play bridge but I will set out in the chapters that follow the basic play which complies mostly with what is called Acol, a widely accepted system. The reference to Acol was the Acol Bridge Club formerly in Acol Road, Hampstead in London NW6 and where the Acol system of bidding was first introduced in 1934.

Following *The Road Across the Bridge*, I plan to retrace my steps across the Bridge and cover all the aspects of the game I covered in my first book but in a different way and also to introduce several other conventions which I have found very useful.

I will give you my thoughts on the bidding and some of the play arising from the hands I will set out. I will suggest leads but will not attempt to set out in detail how the hands should be played. I am just not qualified. I make too many careless and silly mistakes playing the cards to call myself an expert. Far better for you to fathom out the best course of action from experience and you will benefit no end from the many mistakes you will make at the table along the way. What I will try to do as far as I can is to suggest a thought pattern for you to follow. Bridge is not an easy game to learn but get the basics on board and you will have many hours of enjoyment with friends.

I also plan to say a few words about those Rules of Bridge which crop up regularly and which are often a 'grey area' in the minds of many players.

By the way – the reference to those trousers. You can guess who asked the question. Yes it's my wife Margaret. Putting you in the picture about 'those trousers', they are the ones I wear around the house and the ones I could wear whilst out on my bicycle but not trousers, it seems, I should ever consider wearing to Bridge for example. I don't just have one pair of *'those trousers'*, in fact I have several and whilst I am wearing one pair at the moment, another pair are occupying half the surface of a wooden trunk in the bedroom and which were, this morning, the subject of another enquiry. I must say that Margaret is very polite when she wishes to ask a question because the enquiry is often prefixed, as it was this morning, by the question *"can I ask you a question"* and without waiting for an answer *"can you tell me when you propose to put 'those trousers' in the bedroom in the wash."* I won't bore you with the answer.

There are several types of Bridge but three popular types are Duplicate, Rubber and Chicago. Throughout this book, whenever I have mentioned club Bridge I will be relating to Duplicate Bridge where the cards are pre-dealt at the outset into plastic trays which move from table to table as each round is played.

As in the first book, there will be some interruptions throughout this second tutorial which may have nothing whatsoever to do with Bridge. I'm a bit of a butterfly when it comes to writing and whatever comes to mind at the time could well end up on the page and may even interrupt an explanation of the bidding and play and if that happens and interrupts your train of thought then I apologise in advance.

I played bridge at one of my local clubs twice last Wednesday. Once in the afternoon with my German friend Ingrid who is 60 plus and again in the evening with my Swedish friend Karin who is 60 minus and that's about as international as I get. The afternoon session was a bit of a disaster but we didn't finish bottom so that was a plus. I made a silly little bidding error on one hand and my play of the cards on another hand was abysmal and not what one would expect from a chap who is trying put together a second bridge tutorial.

My appalling performance in the afternoon was forgotten soon after I started playing with Karin in the evening. Better rephrase that. Sitting opposite Karin in the evening I soon forgot the troubles of the afternoon and play went smoothly, my making only one silly little error of judgement which was expensive but in spite of that we ended up in first place out of 17 tables. Let me tell you that I was playing at The Worthing Bridge Club where the general standard of play is quite high so coming top is of some significance. So, all in all the day ended satisfactorily.

For me, Bridge is no different from any other pursuit when participants are trying their best to succeed. Most of us always try to do our best be it Golf, Snooker, Tennis, whatever and are disappointed with our performance if we achieve less than is acceptable to us but that surely motivates us into an endeavour to do better the next time. We all have days when things don't go quite as planned. I remember well in my early days of Bridge, the many times I would drive home from the West Sussex Bridge Club at 11 o'clock at night, having made some stupid mistakes and then not being able to get to sleep through those daft errors going round and round in my mind. It was not long before I realised the futility of worrying about what was to me after all, only a game.

Some specimen hands will be set out in pages that follow. Each bid will be discussed, a suggestion as to what card to lead and why and sometimes the thoughts of the Declarer and the Defenders after the first card is led. That's the intention anyway so let's see how things progress. By the way the abbreviations **LHO** and **RHO** stand for left and right hand opposition and some of the other Bridge terminology is as follows:

Honour cards - The Aces, Kings, Queens and Jacks. A Jack is often called a knave.

Majors/minors - Spades/Hearts majors. Diamonds/Clubs - minors.

Hand – The 13 cards you are dealt at the outset.

Trick – The one card from each of four players in one round.

Void – Not having cards in a particular suit.

Bidding – As in an auction.

Bidding boxes – Containers for bidding cards.

On lead – The first person to lead to a trick.

Make – It's a Bridge term for shuffling the cards.

A fit – Having at least 8 cards in a suit between your hand and your partner's hand opposite.

Book – The first six tricks made which do not count towards a score.

Game – In a no-trump contract game is bidding and achieving three tricks above the 'book' of six tricks. In a contract in a major suit a game is the bidding of and achieving four tricks above the 'book' of six tricks and in a minor suit, game is the bid of and achieving five tricks above the 'book' of six tricks.

Ruff – A Bridge term for trumping.

Alert – When partner makes an unnatural bid up to a certain level of bidding then you must indicate the fact by – an alert or an announcement (to be explained later).

Finesse – An endeavour to win a trick with a lower card.

Yarborough – A hand containing no honour cards. It is said that the odds against both members of a partnership receiving a Yarborough are 546 million to one although a Yarborough in one of the partnership hands is fairly common.

Vulnerability – In Rubber Bridge the partnership who win 100 points before the other partnership, become what is known as vulnerable and in Duplicate Bridge the vulnerability is already determined and confirmed on the tray of pre-dealt cards. In Chicago Bridge the vulnerability is normally set out on the score cards. In Duplicate and Chicago Bridge, when vulnerable, the partnership earn more bonus points for making game but as in Rubber Bridge, loose more points when the contract fails.

The Revoke – Not following suit when you have a card in the led suit in your hand.

Chicane – A hand without any trumps.

Sacrifice – Bidding a game contract with little expectation of making that contract but by going down, losing fewer points than letting the other side play and win in their contract.

Who is writing this book – me or the computer? Two lines above I'd typed <u>losing less points</u> and this clever dick computer of mine thought better and underlined the last two words in green. It seems the computer prefers the word fewer to the word less so <u>losing fewer points</u> it is. It'll be telling me next how to play Bridge. No comment.

The Declarer – The player who first named the denomination (the suit or no-trumps) of the final contract and that title is set once the first card is led and faced by the player sitting on that player's left hand side.

Dummy Hand – The hand of cards placed on the table by the partner of the Declarer, once the first card is faced.

The Defenders – The players who are the opponents of the Declarer.

Immediate Seat – is the position at the Bridge table immediately beyond and on the left of the Declarer.

Balancing Seat – is the position at the Bridge table immediately before and on the Declarer's right hand side.

Limit bids – are bids that correctly or very nearly reflect the full strength of your hand and they include
- Any game bid
- The majority of no-trump bids.
- Raises in partner's suit to any level.
- Any time a suit is bid for the second time at any level.
- Jump overcalls.
- Pre-emptive opening and overcalls.

A Double - a <u>take-out Double</u> asking partner to bid something – or a <u>Penalty Double</u> when the Doubler hopes to defeat the contract. The difference is set out within the chapter on Doubles.

A Rescue Bid – A rescue bid will normally follow a Penalty Double by the opposition after a bid by the other partnership. It is simply a bid of a suit to remove the Double which does not remove the opportunity for the rescue bid to be Doubled.

The Wriggle – is a bid in an attempt to find another contract after a threatening bid by the opposition – often a Penalty Double.

A Forcing Bid – implied by the convention used or under the agreement of the two partners, it is a bid requesting partner to bid something and not to pass unless there is an intervening bid.

Now some not so serious definitions.

Rabbit – An inexperienced player.

Rattlesnake – A 4441 hand distribution of cards.

Rock Crusher – A very powerful hand.

A Swan – A 7411 hand distribution of cards.

Train Tickets – A holding of very poor cards. Presumably what you would be given for travelling to Yarborough.

Kamikaze No-Trump – Opening 1nt with 9-11 points.

Apricot Sundae – A two suiter of Hearts and Diamonds.

Devil's Bedpost – The Four of Clubs

Kibitzer –A person who watches Bridge play from the sidelines.

The Curse of Scotland – The Nine of Diamonds.

Dustbin Bid – a 1nt response to partner's suit opening when no alternative bid is either suitable or available.

Just a Few Simple Rules

Bridge is a very pleasant and intriguing game and as in most other games the defeat of your opposition should be your aim. Always be very polite in your endeavour to defeat and if successful, have very sympathetic body language when you tell the opposition how unlucky they were.

Never criticise your partner at the table except if your partner's name is Margaret and your name is Bryan. Why Margaret should think it sarcastic when I suggest at the table that perhaps a trump should have been played to win that trick, I do not know and the other times when I politely point out to Margaret that we are playing in a suit contract and had she forgotten that such and such suit was the trump suit. *"I know darling your Ace won the trick and well done for that but the 8 you had in your hand would have served the same purpose and you could have saved your Ace to trap the King which subsequently made a trick – my darling."*

Always count your cards before looking at them when collecting them from the table to ensure you have 13 and then count them again when your fan is spread out to make sure the 13 cards are in view. It is so frustrating when you find an honour card was hidden and you have passed in the bidding process when you could have opened the bidding, overcalled or supported your partner.

When you are the Declarer and the first card is led and your partner puts a poor Dummy hand on the table you must be enthusiastic and thank your partner and you can even add a pleasing comment as to how the Dummy hand looks even though you are disappointed at what has been placed on the table opposite. Never be downhearted about the Dummy hand even though your partner's bidding has proved to be somewhat suspect. The opposition want you to be disappointed and dejected so why let them know you are less than very happy.

It is very bad manners to start collecting the cards as they are being dealt. Wait until the dealer has finished and then collect your cards and as a matter of course count them <u>before looking at them</u>. If you do not have 13 cards then make your discovery known to the dealer.

In Bridge there are Laws, to which players should adhere in clubs and in competitions and to give you an idea of the number of rules, The Laws of Duplicate Contract Bridge are set out in a little book containing almost 100 pages to which tome the Director (the person in charge of proceedings at the Bridge club) will often refer if there is a problem at the table which cannot be resolved without reference. The most common infringements in my experience being the following:

Revoking.
Passing out of rotation.
Bidding out of rotation.
Change of call.
Insufficient bid.
Opening lead out of turn.

I joke not when I tell you that the giving of unauthorised information by hesitation and body movements can be treated as infringements of Bridge Law and even the location of the empty plastic card tray on the table during play of Duplicate Bridge can be incorrect and on that particular point I will comment at length later as a result of personal experience.

No, on second thoughts I won't delay – no time like the present. I'll tell you now about that empty card tray incident which caused me some minor irritation at the time because the player who caused the situation was so pedantic by insisting the rules were obeyed to the letter and talking about letter, this is what I wrote to the editor of one of the popular Bridge magazines and the reply of his expert follows.

Dear Sir,

When I am the Declarer, I like to move the empty card tray towards me to a position about six inches from the edge of the table leaving enough room for played cards to be placed between the card tray and the edge of the table.

The other day, the opening card was led and I dragged the empty card tray towards me and the lady on my right, sitting north, took the tray and placed it back in the centre of the table. I stated my wish to have the tray nearer me thus making good space for the Dummy hand but she insisted that the empty tray should stay in the centre of the table. Not wishing to be unpleasant I did nothing further. I suspect she was correct, albeit pedantic, but surely if the card tray remains in the centre of the table then it is likely the Dummy hand will be laid in a very restricted area, especially if there is a long suit. I wonder what constitutes the centre of the table.

And the reply came back

Dear Bryan,

Whatever the theory, in practice players often move the trays around and generally compromise. Some do it because they like the Dummy closer to be able to see it better, some do it so that they can reach Dummy to play the cards, though of course they should not be touching the cards.

But while most players are tolerant, there is intolerance in the game and it is growing slightly. If someone demands the card tray should be in the exact centre of the table, then that is what the Law says so I am afraid you should just accept it. Yours truly.

Law 7a of the Bridge Rules clearly states and I quote 'When a board is to be played it is placed in the centre of the table until play is completed'.

If that's the law then the next time I play with one of my friends who is a little short sighted and she becomes the Declarer, I will have to think very carefully where to put Dummy's cards on the table for her to see. With the card tray or the board as it is called, placed in the centre of the table, I will either have to place the Dummy hand between the centralised board and my partner which may not leave too much room for her to table her played cards or between the centralised board and myself which could well cause her problems in seeing what cards are displayed. On the other hand I could drape the Dummy hand across the empty card tray which would distract my partner no end but the undulations in each suit would be quite novel which would give a new meaning to the Declarer's instruction to Dummy as to playing a high card or a low card.

Of course I am being facetious but I'm just emphasising the attitude of some folk who stick rigidly to rules.

I am a member of several Bridge clubs and in each club there is a different level of discipline as to how the Bridge Laws are interpreted. At one club where there is often a non playing Director, the rules are very seriously obeyed by most players and there are always a lot of very serious faces, even between games. At the other clubs a more relaxed atmosphere exists most of the time, which suits me fine. When a playing Director is called, often interrupting her or his game, it is only on occasions when a problem cannot be satisfactorily resolved at the table.

I have to smile to myself when I think of what happened at one club years ago, when one of the opposition players revoked; did not follow suit when a card of the led suit was in hand. When I pointed out the infringement at the end of the play, the elderly gentleman just looked at me knowingly and did nothing. His lady partner's facial expression confirmed the revoke but I let the matter rest because the revoke did not cause us to loose a trick. Normally a trick or two is awarded to the other side but on that occasion it did not matter. Why do I smile to myself? The elderly gentleman in question was the Director for the evening.

I know rules are rules and they are set for a very good reason and that reason I respect. They are designed to set the proper procedures and to provide a sufficient remedy whenever play accidentally, intentionally and inadvertently disturbs the proper course of the game and provides the perpetrator with an unfair advantage. How those rules are interpreted are down to the management committee of the club. Most of the Bridge players with whom I associate, play Bridge at their local Bridge club because they like playing Bridge and they like a pleasant afternoon or evening away from the four walls at home. In competitions then the rules must be strictly adhered and rightly so but for me and most folk I suspect, the strict adherence to the rules can sometimes be a bit of a bore. By the same token I certainly do not want the rules at the local Bridge clubs relaxed to such an extent that the game is spoilt. Moderation with everything.

When considering the Laws of Bridge, you must appreciate there is a vast difference between a friendly game at home with your friends and your favourite tipple by your side and the competitive game of Bridge at the club. When playing Bridge at home or away from a Club situation then many of the Laws can be and are often relaxed. For example when a player bids out of turn or leads a card out of turn then the infringement is often rectified without any further thought and play continues normally.

I am all in favour of good manners at the Bridge table whether playing at home or at the club and when describing the bidding and opening lead formalities, I have mentioned the good mannered and correct procedure which need not be taken on board for games at home or for that matter not often necessarily for games at the local club. They are mentioned because they are part of Bridge etiquette. I refer to any questions prior to the play of the first card, Declarer's 'thank you' when the Dummy hand goes down and the way Declarer indicates to partner which card to play from Dummy. One lady I know, when playing as Declarer, reaches across the table, picks out a card and flips it across to partner and sometimes with new cards, the shiny surface causes the card to slide leaving the Dummy person acting as goalkeeper. This action is of course against the rules.

17

I was just about to open my 2172 page dictionary to look up the word Serendipity which I spotted whilst reading a newspaper article from America about Hilary's weak spots, when the lady who interrupted my train of thought earlier this morning with a very welcome mug of coffee, asked me to do something about her tyres. She did not take kindly to my enquiry as to the tyres on her bike or her spare tyres. The former, of course, how silly of me, because she attends keep fit classes twice a week. I'm now sitting here thinking about those twenty or so ladies prancing about with those body parts not adequately lashed down moving uncontrollably like ferrets inside a sack.

Now where was I? Oh yes. I bought this huge tome several years ago for the princely sum of £8 which represents £1 for every 271 pages which I reckon was fantastic value.

Now Serendipity. I looked up the definition because I needed to be informed. If I asked 10 people in the street what serendipity meant I would probably get one answer, sorry I do not know and nine people would say 'sorry I'm not sure', knowing full well they didn't have a clue. Right – Serendipity. A natural gift for making useful discoveries quite by accident and funnily enough that noun relates to me at the moment. I've just discovered that Bridge champions usually peak in their late 30's so that cuts me out by thirty years.

Now back to some Bridge etiquette that should be exercised at the Bridge Club but not necessarily at home.

After the auction, the player 'on lead' sitting on the left hand side of the Declarer, should draw a card from hand, place it face down on the table or hold it in hand face down, look across to partner with the enquiry, by word or facial expression, as to any questions and irrespective of whether partner has any questions or not that card should be played.

Why questions?

- Firstly - is the lead being made from the correct hand? An advantage to the opposition or the Declarer could easily arise by a lead from the wrong opposition hand. The Declarer has the right to call the Director who will give the Declarer certain options which could be to the Declarer's advantage. For example, the Declarer may demand or ban the lead of that suit from the correct hand. The Declarer also has the opportunity of accepting the 'out of turn' lead and becoming the Dummy.

- Secondly - it does give an opportunity for any bids by the opposition to be clarified.

If there are no questions arising, which is usual, then the first card is faced on the table and if bidding boxes have been used then all the bids are then removed from the table and put away. The card drawn must be played even if questions arise that cause the person on lead to reconsider. At that point the Dummy hand is placed on the table with the trump suit, if applicable, on Dummy's right hand side so that Declarer can view them on the left hand side. Declarer should thank partner.

Questions may be asked throughout the play but there are laid down rules as to when questions can be raised. A player may ask for the meaning of a call:

- At any time during auction when it is the player's turn to call.
- Before selecting the opening lead if player is 'on lead'.
- After the opening lead is face-down if partner is on lead.
- Before the opening lead is faced if player is Declarer.
- At turn to play if player is Declarer or a Defender.

The Declarer may ask about the Defenders' card play agreements:

- Before the opening lead is faced
- At her/his turn to play throughout the play of the hand.

Passing information to your partner other than by the bidding process is unlawful such as holding cards with left hand showing two fingers to indicate two aces and things like that or placing a hand on a part of your body to indicate a particular suit is held. Placing a hand in your lap could indicate something else and so on and with this in mind, best you do not cough however innocently, during the bidding process and take care also that a blink is not construed as being a wink.

In Duplicate Bridge, following the lead of the first card the 'Dummy' person will take instructions from the Declarer in every card movement but in Rubber Bridge the Declarer physically selects a card to be played.   In Duplicate Bridge the Declarer will say what card is to be played unless, of course, the card is obvious because it is the only one left in Dummy but there is an exception. When the first card is led and the Dummy hand goes on the table and there is a singleton of the led suit in the Dummy hand, the Dummy person must not play the card for Declarer until requested. After the first card is laid, the Declarer must have the opportunity of assessing the Dummy hand and when ready to proceed will tell Dummy what card to play even though the card is an obvious singleton. Even if there are two adjacent cards of equal value such as a KQ or 98, the Declarer will still dictate which card is to be played. Dummy must never ever say for example *"Do you want me to play this card?"* with an outstretched finger pointing at or touching a card.

When playing socially then certain Bridge rules and etiquette obviously go by the wayside, because the discipline is not necessary.

The person playing the Dummy hand must not touch any card in anticipation of Declarer's wishes even when it is obvious, from the Dummy view, what card is to be played. If Declarer plays the Ace for example, the 'obvious' card to be played from the Dummy hand, which is normally the lowest card in the suit, must not be touched by Dummy until instructed by the Declarer. The Declarer may require a higher card played in order to keep the lead of that suit subsequently in hand rather than in Dummy. Dummy must never assume.

What Dummy is allowed to do other than twiddle with fingers or a button is to say *'having none partner'* to prevent Declarer from establishing a revoke, when partner shows as being void of a suit. Dummy will not have too much to do but must be careful not to be caught doing a bit of reconnaissance whilst at the Bridge club. Tables are sometimes quite close together and it is often easy to observe cards in the hands of those at the next table if you are idly gazing around whilst partner and opposition are deep in concentration.

At the Bridge club the Dummy person is allowed to leave the table for comfort purposes or for a smoke if that way inclined, which leaves the Declarer having to physically play the Dummy cards but often the opposition assist under Declarer's instruction. Both on the way out and on the return journey to the table, the Dummy person does have a wonderful opportunity to have a surreptitious look at the cards held at the adjacent table and which set of cards are next to be played. Perish the thought. I'm not talking about you or me for that matter but there are players that will do anything to gain an unfair advantage. Also not permissible at the Bridge club, but in order socially, is the Dummy person going round the other side of the table and viewing Declarer's hand.

The Dummy person is not allowed to ask a defender about a possible revoke and must not draw attention to any problem before the hand is over.

I have set out the strict rules as to questions but if your name is Margaret Stephens, then you can raise a question at any time of any person and the question usually raised is *"can you tell me what I'm supposed to do with this hand?"* and *"if I bid 'so and so' what am I telling you?"* Life gets difficult sometimes.

Let's get on with some Bridge.

The first two chapters will cover opening the bidding 1nt and partner's unopposed response. The first chapter will deal with opening bids of 1nt and responding with a balanced hand and chapter two will cover the response to partner's 1nt opening when holding an unbalanced hand. Still on the subject of no-trumps, chapter three deals with card play, leads and bits and pieces.

I mention these three chapters in particular because I'm going to introduce two very popular conventions called Stayman and Transfers. In Bridge a convention is a partnership agreement. It is a bid that asks for information or provides information that is unconnected to the suit that is bid. There are hundreds of conventions but most players enjoy their Bridge using just a few.

The Stayman convention was featured briefly in *The Road Across the Bridge* and I mention the word briefly because I enquired years ago about the Stayman convention from a very experienced club member and the following week I was handed two thick files of foolscap on the subject. Latterly in my last book I mentioned Transfers but did not expand on the convention because I did not want to confuse the reader who would have been confused enough at that stage of tuition.

As the Stayman Convention and the Transfer Convention, correctly named Red Suit Transfers are so popular and I thoroughly recommend them, I have decided to make a separate section for just those two conventions starting on the next page.

Using the conventions is not mandatory but as they are so popular you should know about them even if you and your partner decide not to use them because you will play against other players who use the conventions. Either use Stayman and or Transfers or not and that is a partnership decision. You cannot suddenly decide during a game that the bidding system should change just because it suits your hand. In any event how on earth is your partner going to know?

Stayman and Transfers.

The Stayman Convention - The Stayman conventional bid after partner has opened 1nt is 2c (2 Clubs). It does not mean that you have Clubs in your hand and want to bid Clubs but it is a <u>false bid</u> and asks for information about your partner's hand. The bid requests your partner to tell you about any four card majors in hand. Its purpose is to discover, after partner has opened in no trumps whether a 4-4 *fit* in a major suit exists. You have four or more cards in a major suit, Spades or Hearts or both, yourself and wonder whether your partner also has a four card major because often it is better to play in a major suit where there is a *fit* rather than in a no-trump contract. So you ask the question by bidding 2c which means *"partner do you have a 4 card major?"*

After the Stayman 2c enquiry the replies are as follows:

- 2d – The negative not having a four card major.
- 2h - Having four Hearts (not denying 4 Spades).
- 2s - Having four Spades (denying 4 Hearts)
- Having both Hearts and Spades bid 2h.

In bidding 2c after partner's 1nt opening, you should be prepared for a negative reply of either 2d (no four card major held) or a two level bid in the other major to the one you have in your hand. In this event you can escape to 2nt with 11/12 points or bid 3nt with 13 or more points.

Transfers – firstly. The Red Suit Transfer bid by responder after partner's 1nt opening. The idea is to transfer the play into the stronger hand. Your partner has opened 1nt and you have 10 points or less and an unbalanced hand with five cards in a major and no intervention by the opposition. You would normally bid the major suit as a weak take-out which your partner would leave. With Transfers you do not bid your major suit at the 2 level but the suit immediately below at the 2 level and your partner (the opener) announces 'Hearts' for example after your bid of 2d and 'Spades' after your bid of 2h. So for a weak take-out into say Hearts you would bid 2d and a weak take-out into Spades you would bid 2h. The play is then transferred to the stronger hand and thus the weak hand goes down on the table as the Dummy for everyone to see.

Transfers - Secondly – For want of a better description - **the 'add on' bids** as I call them. After partner's 1nt and no bids by the opposition, holding a balanced hand and 11/12 points you learnt that you would bid 2nt leaving partner to decide what to bid next not knowing whether you had 11 or 12 points. With the commonly accepted 'add on' bids to the Transfer convention, you can now be specific. By bidding 2s after partner's 1nt opening, you confirm exactly 11 points and by bidding 2nt you confirm exactly 12 points. Your partner can then decide with more comfort as to whether 3nt is on, holding that problematic 13 point no-trump hand.

In some partnerships, the 2s bid is for a transfer to a specified minor suit but personally I prefer the 2s bid showing exactly 11 points. If you have a significant number of Clubs or Diamonds and would rather not pass after partner's 1nt opening bid but prefer to be in your minor suit, bid Stayman 2c and whatever partner responds bid Clubs at the 3 level or if your suit is Diamonds then bid 3d or better still pass should your partner reply 2d to your Stayman bid.

If you bid 2c as Stayman then partner must announce 'Stayman' and it is considered to be part of Stayman for the take out into either Clubs or Diamonds. You and your partner must decide what system you will use and stick to it throughout.

Transfers - Thirdly – **Using the Red Suit Transfer system to confirm points and length in a major**. With the above now in mind you can use Transfers to tell partner not only about a five card major suit by bidding 2d or 2h but also that you have 11/12 or 13 points or more. So after partner's opening Int you, holding the hand shown, are able to tell your partner not only that you have 5 Hearts but also that you have 11/12 points. How? After

♠ Q5
♥ K10943
♦ K76
♣ QJ6

partner's 1nt opening you bid 2d showing your Hearts. Your partner announces 'Hearts' and bids 2h. With a weak take-out hand which this is not, you would now pass leaving partner to play 2h, but now after partner's 2h bid you bid 2nt which confirms not only five Hearts, as a result of the previous bid, but also 11/12 points. The bidding went 1nt-2d-2h-2nt. This will now give your partner a better picture of your hand so with say three Hearts in hand and say 13/14 points your partner can consider a game bid in Hearts. Again after 2h transferring to 2s and you have 13 or more points you can bid 3nt which shows game points and at least five Spade cards.

Both Stayman and the Red Card Transfer conventions are used only after a no-trump opening bid. The two conventional transfer bids namely 2d and 2h are normally used when holding an unbalanced hand and linked to these two transfer bids are two popular bids namely 2s and 2nt which are widely used when holding a balanced hand. The four conventional bids have in practice become collectively known as 'Transfers'. I consider the two transfer bids 2d and 2h and what I call the two 'add on' bids namely 2s and 2nt very worthwhile and I am sure you will agree.

You do not have to use these conventional bids. Some folk do and some don't; it is entirely up to you and your partner. I say again, it is entirely up to you and your partner whether you use the popular Stayman and Transfer conventions but if you do, then be sure you and your partner are singing from the same hymn sheet. Conventions are not the be-all and end-all and good card play does count for a lot. I know many Bridge players who regularly achieve good results yet play very few of the enormous number of conventions. There is an Internet site of Bridge conventions and several conventions are highlighted on each of over 57 pages.

In chapter 16 I'm going to mention another very important convention called **Cue Bidding** which makes life somewhat easier when dealing with the Blackwood Ace/King seeking convention also detailed in the same chapter.

Contrary to the Rules but normally Generally Accepted and Common Practices at the Bridge Club

In Duplicate Bridge where the cards are all pre-dealt and placed within trays which move from table to table, each player will play a card to each trick on the section of the table nearest to them. Once the four cards have been played the cards are placed face down vertically on the table section nearest the player as 'winners' or horizontally as 'losers'. Then at the end of the game and say eight of the thirteen tricks have been won then eight cards will be in the vertical position and five laid horizontally. Therefore if there is any dispute as to the number of tricks won, the problem can easily be solved by checking.

So often the Dummy person, for example, will comment to Declarer that a played card is facing the wrong way and one Defender will say the same to the other Defender and sometimes references are made to an opponent that a 'played' card is facing the wrong way.

It is my understanding that players, including the Dummy person should not remind any other player that a 'played' card is facing the wrong way. The reason is simple. If one player has, for example a 'played' card standing up vertically as a winner rather than lying down horizontally as a loser then that 'winner' may cause that person to believe a greater number of tricks have been made thus improving confidence which could effect the way that player is playing. Believing the contract is 'made' the player may chance a finesse which action may not have been risked otherwise.

If you use bidding boxes and you are not the person 'on lead' you must not put your bids away before the first card is led.

Another little irregularity which crops up time and time again

At the auction room where a painting for example is being auctioned, bids are made and the sale is concluded when the auctioneer bangs down his gavel. The person who has been successful in the auction does not then deny having purchased the painting but so often that happens at the Bridge table and an unintentional 'denial' of the bid already made will be shown.

Those of you who have played Bridge will know exactly what I mean because it happens time and time again and nobody says a word. The Declarer has already been established because of the three passes after the last bid, yet the Declarer or partner will say PASS or draw a pass card from the bidding box and place it on the table. You watch the next time you play Bridge how often the bidding will finish like this.

North	East	South	West
1nt	pass	2c	pass
2h	pass	2nt	pass
3nt	pass	pass	pass
PASS			

North has already secured the contract for the partnership by the 3nt bid yet after three passes North then passes.

It happens so often that I expect you may even do it yourself.

Now there's a thought.

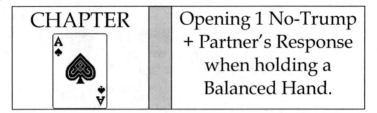

| CHAPTER | Opening 1 No-Trump + Partner's Response when holding a Balanced Hand. |

The Opening 1nt Hand will be Balanced
and have a
12, 13 or 14 High Card Point Window

Called
The Weak No-Trump

The most popular point range in a 1nt opener is 12/14 and is called a <u>weak no-trump</u>. The less popular <u>strong no-trump point range</u> is 16/19 or 17/19. Often used with the strong no-trump is what is called Five Card Majors which is a partnership understanding that on an opening bid in a major suit, at least five cards are held. The system was first introduced into North American tournament bidding in the 50's and opening 1c is often the conventional opening bid, holding opening points but without a five card major. Throughout this book the widely recognised weak no-trump will be used and there will be no further reference to Five Card Majors.

Whenever you play Bridge, if nothing is said then normally the opposition will assume you play the Weak No-Trump but new rules being proposed by the English Bridge Union may dictate that whenever the bid is made the partner should announce 12-14 or 16-19 whatever is applicable. I have found when I play at my local clubs that those partnerships who play the strong no-trump will always announce that fact when they arrive at your table or you at theirs.

A Balanced Hand showing 12-14 points

4333 or 4432 or 5332 shape

No Void or Singleton and No two Doubletons

No Five Card Major
but you may be excused for
bidding 1nt if your major suit
looks like this 76432

Sitting in the 4th position after three passes you can open 1nt holding only 11 points but be careful if vulnerable and remember your partner has passed. Suppose each of the opposition players has 11 points as well then your partner will have only 7 points.

AQ65	♠	AQ	AQ653	AQ	♠	AQ65
J74	♥	J74	J74	Q743	♥	J
K96	♦	K9643	KJ6	KJ	♦	AJ84
QJ5	♣	QJ5	QJ	98653	♣	Q653
Balanced and you should open 1nt		Five card minor suit you can open 1nt	Five card major. <u>Do not</u> open 1nt	Two doubletons. <u>Do not</u> Open 1nt		Singleton. <u>Do not</u> Open 1nt

What the responder does now depends very much on whether a balanced or unbalanced hand is held, whether the Stayman and/or the Transfer conventions have been agreed and of course, on the number of points held in hand. This chapter deals with responses with balanced hands.

Responding to 1nt holding a balanced hand.
Holding less than 11 points <u>you pass</u> even if you hold AKQJ.
Holding 11/12 points you bid 2nt.
Holding 13 /18 points you bid 3nt.
Action holding more than 18 points will be discussed later.
but
Holding 11 or more points and a four card major or both
then consider the Stayman convention as explained earlier.

29

Very Important - Only use Stayman when you have an escape into 2nt holding at least 11 points should you not get a good answer <u>except</u> when you have low points and <u>five cards in both majors.</u> Look at the situation holding this hand after partner has opened 1nt.

♠	98753
♥	Q9532
♦	J6
♣	9

Holding this hand you should bid 2c – Stayman and if partner bids 2h or 2s you pass but if partner bids the negative 2d then you would bid 2h. Use Stayman to get into the best major rather than the weak take-out bid and maybe into the wrong major. This way you have a good chance of finding the best major.

If you use Stayman and I expect you will, then be very sure that you have discussed it with your partner at the outset because if you have not agreed to the convention and you bid 2c after your partner's 1nt and your partner passes, do not blame your partner. You should see the smug look of delight on the faces of the opposition when a convention has not been agreed or been forgotten. You've got two little clubs but 11 points and four Heart cards. You bid the Stayman 2c and to your horror your partner passes leaving you to fight the 2c contract when you should have been in a major game. Then you see your partner's hand go on the table and don't those three Clubs headed by the Jack look pathetic.

If you use the Transfer convention then after your partner's no-trump opening bid, your bid of:

- 2d asks partner to bid 2h
- 2h asks partner to bid 2s
- 2s tells partner you have exactly 11 points
- 2nt tells partner you have exactly 12 points.

In the two sets of hands that follow, I will respond without using the conventional Transfer bids and then show the response using Transfers and you will be able to see the difference. I stress, you do not have to use these conventions and many players manage happily without and it is entirely up to you and your partner. You must decide at the outset of any Bridge session whether or not the conventional bids are going to be used.

30

Opener	Stayman agreed but not Transfers			Responder
1nt	QJ93	♠	A6	2nt (showing 11/12 pts)
	KJ4	♥	Q83	
pass (poor 13 points)	J843	♦	AQ72	
	KQ	♣	9852	

Opener	Stayman and Transfers agreed			Responder
1nt	QJ93	♠	A6	2nt (showing 12 points)
	KJ4	♥	Q83	
3nt	J843	♦	AQ72	pass
	KQ	♣	9852	

If your partner has opened 1nt and your RHO has intervened with a bid, then normally the Stayman & Transfer conventions are not used unless, by partnership agreement, another bid is used. In some partnerships, if the RHO opposition player has interfered with a 2c overcall, (conventional or natural) then a Double will suffice as meaning a Stayman enquiry.

If you are the no-trump opener and your RHO has bid after your partner has used either the Stayman or Transfer Convention, a reply to either convention often cannot be given but nevertheless the reason for partner bidding the convention is taken on board.

The partnership has agreed to use both Stayman and Transfers.

Opener bids 1nt.	A97	♠	Q5	Responder bids 2d.
	K10	♥	AJ862	
Opener rebids 2h.	973	♦	KJ5	2nt
	KQ763	♣	852	
pass.				

Same opening 1nt and response 2d but this time the responder has another bid in mind to show those 11 points. The opener rebids 2h as requested by the responder's Transfer bid but now the responder bids 2nt which confirms not only 5 Heart cards already confirmed by the 2d Transfer request but also 11/12 points. With only 12 points and only two Hearts the opener will do nothing but pass.

An Invitation or a Request

If you have opened 1nt, do not bid again
unless your partner <u>Requests or Invites</u> you to bid.

An invitation by your partner –
- If you have not agreed Stayman or Transfers, a 2nt response is an <u>invitation</u> by your partner to bid to 3nt because your partner holds 11 /12 points.
- If you have agreed Transfers, a 2s response from partner will confirm exactly 11 points and be an <u>invitation</u> to bid to game as will a 2nt response holding exactly 12 points.

A request by your partner –
- If you have agreed Stayman then a 2c response will <u>request</u> you to bid a four card major or reply the negative 2d. If you have 4 cards in both majors, bid 2h.
- If you have agreed Transfers then partner's 2d bid will <u>request</u> that you bid 2h or partner's 2h bid will <u>request</u> that you bid 2s.

In the several sets of hands that follow in this chapter and chapters 2 and 3 also dealing with no-trumps you will notice I have indicated whether either Stayman or Transfers or both have been agreed. The subsequent bidding may not feature either convention and the reason is that the partnership agrees to use or not to use the conventions at the outset of the Bridge session. On many hands featured, the agreed conventions simply cannot or should not be used.

Opener	Stayman agreed but not Transfers				Responder
Opening bid 1nt	AJ5	♠	K874	2c (Stayman)	
	8752	♥	A94		
Rebid – 2h	KQ3	♦	874	2nt	
	Q74	♣	AJ5		
Pass					

Having 11/12 points and a 4 card major, responder bids Stayman 2c seeking a Spade fit. The 2h reply from partner does not deny four Spades because holding 4 cards in both majors the Hearts are bid first. Responder's reply to opener's 2h rebid is 2nt confirming no interest in Hearts but 11/12 points. The opener knows that partner, having bid 2c seeking a four card major has 4 Spades but not four Hearts hence the reply of 2nt. The opener with only 12 points passes because there are not enough points in the two hands for game.

See the difference in bidding – opener has 4 cards in both majors

Opener	Stayman agreed but not Transfers				Responder
Opening bid 1nt	AJ52	♠	K874	2c (Stayman)	
	8752	♥	A94		
Rebid – 2h	KQ3	♦	87	2nt	
	Q7	♣	AJ53		
Third bid - 3s				pass	

Again responder seeks a fit by bidding 2c and again the reply is 2h, bidding the lower of two four card majors. The responder is still not interested in Hearts and replies 2nt showing 11/12 points. The opener knows that the responder has four Spades because of the 2c major seeking bid and having ignored the 2h reply, by bidding 2nt, must hold 4 Spades. With only 12 points in hand and 11/12 points opposite evidenced by the 2nt bid, the opener will bid 3s. The responder will pass because partner has just confirmed a minimum hand and had the opener wanted to bid to game, with all the information at hand then 4s would have been bid. The 3s bid by the opener is certainly not invitational.

Now the opener has 2 more points

Opener	Stayman agreed but not Transfers			Responder
Opening bid 1nt	AJ52	♠	K874	2c (Stayman)
	Q752	♥	A94	
Rebid – 2h	KQ3	♦	87	2nt
	Q7	♣	AJ53	
Third bid – 4s				

Knowing there are four Spades opposite by partner having bid 2c, seeking a four card major and ignoring the 2h reply, the opener with maximum points can now comfortably bid to game in Spades – 4s knowing about the fit in Spades and at least 25 points having had 11/12 points confirmed by the responder's 2nt bid.

Now look what happens when the partnership have agreed to use both Stayman and Transfers when the responder with 11/12 points does not hold four cards in a major.

Opener	Stayman and Transfers agreed			Responder
Opening bid 1nt	AJ52	♠	Q74	2s (showing 11 points)
	K875	♥	943	
Rebid – 2nt	Q3	♦	A87	pass
	Q73	♣	AJ85	

Simple enough. Opener showing 12-14 points and responder showing exactly 11 points.

Opener	Stayman and Transfers agreed			Responder
Opening bid 1nt	AJ52	♠	K74	2nt (showing 12 points)
	K875	♥	943	
Rebid – 3nt	K3	♦	A87	pass
	Q73	♣	AJ85	

This time the opener does not have to wrestle with the decision as whether to go to game holding that difficult 13 point hand. The responder has replied 2nt and with Transfers agreed, the opener knows there are exactly 12 points across the way and with 13 points in hand, is relaxed about bidding to game.

Responding to 1nt with a <u>balanced</u> hand & Opener's rebid.

With less than 11 points and a balanced hand you <u>pass</u>.

Responder	Opener's Rebid
With <u>11/12 points</u> and a four card major bid 2c (Stayman). If partner replies 2d or not in your major then rebid 2nt. If your partner replies in your major suit then bid major at the three level which will tell your partner that you have four cards in that major and 11 or 12 points. If you have agreed to the Transfer convention then bid 2s showing exactly 11 points and 2nt showing exactly 12 points but you may care to bid 2c Stayman holding a four card major.	Reply to Stayman. 2d negative no four card major or bid 4 card major. Bid 2h with both majors. If responder bids 2nt then with good 13pts or 14 points bid 3nt but with 12 points pass. If you respond 2h to partner's 2c Stayman bid and then your partner bids 2nt or 3nt you know your partner has four spades. If partner has bid 2s you will reply 2nt holding 12/13 points but holding 14 points bid 3nt. If partner has bid 2nt then with 12pts pass but with 13/14 bid to game – 3nt.

Responder	Opener's rebid
With <u>13/18 points</u> bid Stayman if relevant then bid 4 of major with a reply in your major or 3nt with negative reply. Without a four card major then bid 3nt straight away. If you have bid 2c Stayman and your partner replies 2d or not in your major then bid 3nt. If your partner replies in your major then bid to game in that major.	After responder's Stayman enquiry and then responder's bid of 3nt the opener will decide whether to stay in 3nt or bid game in the major. If the responder has bid 2c and then 3nt to your 2h reply then the opener will know that 4 spades are held.

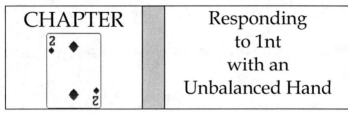

| CHAPTER 2 | | Responding to 1nt with an Unbalanced Hand |

Your partner has opened the bidding with 1nt and the lady on your right hand side has passed. Holding a balanced hand and less than 11 points you would pass. Remember a balanced hand means no void, singleton or two doubletons.

The next sentence is set out in larger print for Margaret's benefit.

If you are not balanced and have less than 11 points then you must take out into your longest suit. It's called a Weak Take-Out.

We were playing with our good friends Sue and John the other week and Sue opened 1nt and we all passed leaving Sue in a 1 no-trump contract with me on lead. I was not able to lead the top of an internal high run but I did hold J10973 of Diamonds and after drawing the J♦ from my hand and holding it face down, I enquired of John as to any questions and after a gentle shake of his head, I placed the card face up on the table. Margaret put her thirteen cards on the table and there it was with the emphasis very much on the word - it. It - was the 5 of Diamonds and I mean - it. The lonesome 5 of Diamonds. Also on the table were five Hearts, four Clubs and three Spades, a total of 9 points.

At this point I should give you some background. Several years ago Margaret and her good friend Sue, yes the same Sue, attended two twenty week Bridge lesson sessions at about £80 per session and Margaret has since had scores of lessons from me on the basics of Bridge and I emphasise the word basics. Margaret has openly admitted that she will never excel in Bridge and if she really has to play she prefers to play socially with someone with whom she is comfortable. Margaret is comfortable playing with Sue and I am reliably informed that Sue is of the same mind playing opposite Margaret. John and I do have to be a little careful because often we feel that at any moment their Bridge playing days will draw suddenly to a close.

As a Defender I was pleased to see that singleton Diamond on the table following my lead against Sue's 1 no-trump contract but as Margaret's teacher for many years, following her class-room lessons I was .....what's the word? Dumfounded will do. The contract went three tricks down and following John's announcement that we were 2500 points ahead at that stage, there was another announcement by the two ladies almost in concert. '*Who cares, it's only a game.*' You now understand exactly what John and I have to put up with.

Your partner has opened 1nt and you have a balanced hand and less than 11 points then <u>you pass</u>. If you are unbalanced with less than 11 points then <u>you must bid</u> your longest suit as a weak take-out but there is an exception if your longest suit is Clubs. If you have say five or six run of the mill Clubs then just bite the bullet and pass. Your partner will understand but if the Clubs are significant then bid 2c (Stayman) and then whatever your partner replies, bid 3c and that should be that. You cannot bid 3c straight away because your partner will think you hold more than 10 points.

I have already mentioned the system of Red Card Transfers where you, the unbalanced responder, after partner's bid of 1nt, transfer the play of a major into your partner's hand by bidding 2d for play in Hearts and 2h for play in Spades. When the unbalance is caused by length in a minor you cannot Transfer into a minor unless you have an arrangement with your partner. What you have to do when holding less than 11 points is to either pass your partner's 1nt bid or with significant holdings bid 2c (Stayman) and then bid your suit at the 3 level and your partner will understand. If your partner replies the negative 2d, if your suit is Diamonds you simply pass.

What if you are unbalanced and not so weak? Your partner has bid 1nt and you have 11-18pts. You know your partner has 12/14 points. Holding 11/18pts yourself, you have in mind game in a suit or in no trumps. If you have 4 or more cards in a major then bid Stayman and with a reply not in your major and with 11/12pts bid 2nt but 3nt with 13 or more points. If the reply is positive 2h or 2s then bid your major at the 3 level holding 11/12 points or go to game 4h or 4s holding 13 or more points.

Holding 11/18 points go to 4h or 4s with good six card major.

With length in either minor suit just bid the suit at the 3 level and leave the rest to the opener who will probably bid 3nt depending upon his or her strength.

Opener	Stayman and Transfers agreed			Responder
Opening bid 1nt	J875	♠	10	2d
	K6	♥	Q9754	
2h	AQ76	♦	932	
	K87	♣	J964	pass

Transfers have been agreed. The responder hand is unbalanced and thus not suitable for no-trumps and the 2d bid merely asks partner to bid 2h and that will be the end of the conversation.

Opener	Stayman and Transfers agreed			Responder
Opening bid 1nt	32	♠	98654	2h
	AQ7	♥	8532	
2s	K64	♦	9732	
	KQ983	♣	void	pass

A Yarborough, wildly unbalanced and length in Spades so with the Transfer convention agreed the play is transferred to the opener's stronger hand. The opener complies with partner's request and then the responder has the opportunity of bidding again to continue the 'conversation' or pass as has happened in this case.

Now the responder has a choice of action and has to decide which road should be taken to best tell partner about the response hand.

In the two sets of hands that follow, the partners have agreed to play both Stayman and Transfers. The responder, who is not weak, has two options. To proceed on the Stayman route in the hope of finding a Heart fit or proceeding on the Transfer route by telling partner straight away that five Hearts are held and then confirming the 11/12 points.

Choice 1 – Responder decides to proceed on the Transfer route.

Opener	Stayman and Transfers agreed			Responder
Opening 1nt	10975	♠	AK	2d
	K6	♥	QJ754	
2h (transfer)	AQ76	♦	932	2nt (11/12 points)
	A87	♣	J96	
3nt				

Responder tells partner about the unbalanced hand and the length in Hearts by bidding 2d requesting a bid of 2h and then afterwards tells partner about the 11/12 points by bidding 2nt. The opener now knows that partner has at least five Hearts and 11/12 points. Had the responder 13 points then 3nt would have been bid showing at least five Hearts and 13 or more points. The opener holds a fairly good 13 point hand and with knowledge now gained, bids to game – 3nt hoping that some of partner's 11/12 points are in the Spade suit.

Choice 2 – Responder decides to proceed on the Stayman route when the same result is achieved.

Opener	Stayman & Transfers agreed			Responder
Opening 1nt	10975	♠	AK	2c (Stayman)
	K6	♥	QJ754	
2s (reply to Stayman)	AQ76	♦	932	2nt (11/12 points)
	A87	♣	J96	
3nt				

This situation is where 4s is bid by the opener by implication. The responder, after using the Stayman convention, ignores partner's Heart response and bids no-trumps which implies holding 4 Spades.

The partnership has agreed to use Stayman but not Transfers.

Opener bids 1nt.	K843	♠	AJ76	Responder bids 2c
	Q863	♥	J	
Opener rebids 2h	Q5	♦	K1074	Responder rebids 3nt
	KQ6	♣	A985	
Opener rebids 4s.				Responder passes.

The opener has 12 points and a reasonably balanced hand but a little concerned about the doubleton Diamonds.

The responder has enough points to bid the 3nt, knowing there are at least 12 points opposite. Holding that four card major the responder bids Stayman 2c hoping for a Spade reply when 4s can be bid or a Heart reply satisfying the Heart shortage in hand when 3nt can be bid. Either way the responder does not care because of those 13 points but if opener responds with the negative 2d then 3nt will be bid irrespective of the worrying singleton Heart. The responder will take comfort in the fact that there are at least 12 points opposite and a good chance of partner having one or two Heart honours.

After responder's 2c bid the opener rebids 2h. Holding four cards in both majors the <u>Hearts must be bid first</u> and that would be the case even if the Hearts were 9643 and the Spades AKJ8. The responder is happy with the reply satisfying the Heart shortage in hand and happily bids 3nt but that is not the end of the bidding.

Why did the responder bid 2c and then ignore the opener's Heart reply and bid 3nt confirming game points? To bid Stayman, the responder must have at least one four card major and to have asked for a major and then ignored the reply and bid 3nt does confirm game points and four Spades.

With four Spade cards in hand and knowledge that partner is strong enough for game, having bid 3nt, the opener finishes off in 4s. The responder would not have bid 2c without at least one four or more card major.

Extended Stayman.

You are unbalanced and have five cards in both majors. You have responded 2c to partner's 1nt opening and have received a negative reply – 2d. Your partner must have a least one major with three cards when you can finish in the major with the combined best holding. You bid 3d after partner's negative 2d and that's Extended Stayman. Your partner will reply in the best major at the three level leaving you to decide on game or not.

Two examples of Extended Stayman.

Opener	Stayman & Transfers agreed				Responder
1nt	K74	♠	J8632	2c (Stayman)	
	A3	♥	K9862		
2d (negative)	KQ74	♦	Void	3d (extended Stayman)	
3s	J862	♣	Q95	pass	

The responder hand with that void is certainly not suitable for a no-trump contract but with five cards in both majors, the responder hopes to find a major fit to finish at the 2 level but is disappointed when the 2c Stayman enquiry results in a negative reply. Obviously the responder cannot leave partner's 2d bid standing and knowing partner must have at least one 3 card major, having opening 1nt, now bids the conventional 3d – Extended Stayman and leaves partner's 3s reply as the contract.

Now the responder hand is similar but a little stronger and partner having confirmed 3 Spade cards is relaxed about a game in Spades.

Opener	Stayman & Transfers agreed				Responder
1nt	K74	♠	A8632	2c (Stayman)	
	A3	♥	K9862		
2d (negative)	KQ74	♦	void	3d (extended Stayman)	
3s	J862	♣	A95	4s.	

Responding to 1nt with an <u>unbalanced</u> hand & Opener's Rebid.

Responder	Opener's Rebid
<u>With less than 11 points</u> bid longest suit at 2 level (not Clubs) – a weak take-out.	Opener will pass.
Length in minor (6 or more) go Stayman route then 3 or your minor.	Opener will answer Stayman
If you have agreed Transfers then bid 2d or 2h as applicable then pass reply.	Reply 2h or 2s

<u>11/12 points</u> -Stayman with 4 card major	Reply to Stayman.
With reply in your major, bid at the 3 level otherwise bid 2nt	With good 13 points or 14 points will bid to game.
Holding long minor bid suit at 3 level.	Discretionally leave or bid 3nt.
If you have agreed Transfers then show 5 cards in major by bidding 2d or 2h and then 2nt after partner has transferred.	Opener will know partner has five cards in major and 11/12 points and will either pass or bid to game.

<u>With 13/18 points</u> bid Stayman if relevant and with a reply in your major bid to game or if negative bid 3nt.	Reply to Stayman. Opener has nothing more to say.
If you have agreed to Transfers show 5 cards in major by bidding 2d or 2h and then 3nt after partner has transferred.	Opener will decide. Pass 3nt or bid to game in major. Opener will know responder has at least five cards in the major + game points.
If you have not agreed the Transfer convention then holding five cards in a major and 13/18 points bid major at 3 level and leave the game decision to your partner	The bid at the 3 level by responder is a forcing bid and the opener must decide on game, whether in no-trumps or in responder's suit
With six good cards in a major then bid straight to game.	Opener has nothing more to say

<u>With 13/18 points and your long suit is a minor</u> – Obviously game points but what game? Game in the minor where you need 11 tricks or game in 3nt when you only need 9 tricks. With no over-tricks in either contract the score is the same. Look at your hand. Is there a shortage in a major? If so bid Stayman 2c and see if partner's reply satisfies that shortage in which case bid 3nt.

I had this hand dealt and my partner opened 1nt.
16 points and very unbalanced. What was I to do?
I took the logical course of action. In my partner's hand across the way there were 12-14 points and where would a majority of those points be located?
I bid stop 3nt and my partner made 10 tricks.

♠	K63
♥	3
♦	AQ863
♣	AK53

It stands to reason.

If your partner makes a Stayman enquiry then your partner will have at least one four card major and at least 11 points unless your partner has:

- a). low points and significant length in a minor and wants to end up in that minor or
- b). low points and five cards in both majors and after your 2d negative reply will bid the best major or will pass if you have replied in a major.

If you have replied 2d or 2h to the Stayman enquiry and your partner then bids:

- 2nt – you know your partner has 4 Spades and 11/12 points.
- 3nt - you know partner has 4 Spades and 13 or more points.

If your partner bids Stayman after your 1nt opening bid, then your partner will have an escape should your partner not like your reply.

It stands to reason.

CHAPTER	With No-Trumps in Mind
	What to lead
	Notes on Play
	+ Some Bits and Pieces

Opening Lead against a no-trump contract. Lead from your longest and strongest. Avoid leading suits that have been bid by the opposition. Consider leading a high card in a suit bid by your partner during the auction. If you hold any of the sequence of cards outlined in the following A and B situations then lead the card suggested otherwise the fourth highest as shown in situation C when the Rule of Eleven (to be explained shortly) comes into play.

A. The top of an <u>internal</u> high sequence.

Note the first high internal sequence in spades has the 10 missing and the second sequence in Hearts, the 9 is missing. QJ9 and J108 are still considered to be unbroken sequences in spite of the missing cards because the missing cards can easily be captured by a lead of the suit through Declarer.

AQJ93 – lead the Queen
KJ1082 – lead the Jack
Q10984 – lead the ten

The first of these three examples is a wonderful sequence to hold. If the King does not fall, <u>do not</u> lead again but wait until your partner is hopefully able to subsequently lead that suit back to you when capital will be made. If your partner leads a Queen and you have the King and one other card then play the King to <u>unblock</u> and lead a lower card in the suit back through Declarer.

44

If you have an unbroken internal sequence, if the trick is not taken then continue with the next card down in the sequence.

If your partner leads an honour card then you know the card will be the top card of a high sequence and your partner will also hold the card immediately below.

B. Leading a top card of a high sequence

| Lead the Ace | Lead the King | Lead the Queen | Lead the Jack |

If the higher card(s) do not appear then keep on leading from the top until they do in order to establish the suit.

C. The fourth highest card in longest suit and the **Rule of Eleven**
K10873 – lead the 7
J9752 – lead the 5
Q863 – lead the 3

Obviously when the fourth highest is led it is not the top of any high sequence so here the **Rule of Eleven** (see examples on next page) can be considered by both the Declarer and the partner of the person on lead. If the fourth highest card is led, take the card number from 11 and the answer is the number of cards higher than the card led in the other three hands. You can then decide what higher cards, if any, are held in the opposition hand and play your card accordingly.

If you hold two four cards suits and one looks like K872 and the other looks like 9742 then lead the fourth highest of the 9742, the 2, because you are more likely to win the king in the first suit, if the suit is not led.

An example of the **Rule of Eleven** where the <u>Declarer</u> gains the advantage by considering the Rule.

```
              AQ9
               N
   KJ862   W       E   543
               S
              107
```

South is Declarer– no-trump Contract.

West will lead the 6 being the fourth highest from long suit. Declarer does the calculation. 6 from 11 = 5. There are five cards above the 6 in the hands of North, East and South. Therefore if West had led the fourth highest there cannot be any card above the 6 in East's hidden hand because the five cards are in the North and South hands. Declarer is relaxed at playing either the 9 from Dummy or the 10 in hand to win the trick rather than the Ace or the Queen in Dummy.

An example of the **Rule of Eleven** where the <u>Defenders,</u> gain the advantage by considering the Rule.

```
              A96
               N
   KJ85    W       E   Q107
               S
              432
```

West leads the 5, the fourth highest. East calculates 11 – 5 = 6. Six cards above the 5 in the remaining three hands. East can see three in hand and three in Dummy so there cannot be a card above the 5 in the hidden South hand. Therefore if the 9 is played from Dummy there is no need for East to play the Queen to win the trick; the 10 will suffice. If the 6 is played from Dummy then East's 7 will win the trick.

Get into the habit of running through the Rule of Eleven when a non honour card is led because whilst it is more often than not of little use you will be delighted on those few occasions when the calculation comes up trumps so to speak. Be careful though because if you find that there is only one card above the card led in the hidden hand you will have no idea as to the value of that card.

Care though, the lead of a non honour card will not always be, but I have found that more often than not, it is the fourth highest. After a non honour card has been led you can always ask the partner of the person on lead whether the card led is likely to be the fourth highest.

Look at another situation when it is the <u>Declarer</u> who takes the advantage from considering the Rule of Eleven.

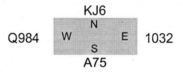

                        KJ6
                         N
         Q984   W   E   1032
                         S
                        A75

West leads the 4 and Declarer considers 11 – 4 = 7 cards above the 4 in the remaining three hands. There are six cards above the 4 in the North and South hands so there must be only 1 card above the 4 in East's hand. Declarer plays low from Dummy and East plays the 10 and South the Ace. Declarer is now pretty sure that the Queen is sitting in West's hand which is covered by the King in Dummy and that Jack in the Dummy hand now looks rather attractive.

It's a lovely feeling

You calculate the Rule of Eleven and
take the trick with a nine when you
would otherwise have played a King.
A grand feeling -
almost smug perhaps.

What card would you lead
defending a no-trump contract?

a). Ace,   b). Queen   c). Nine

Answer is of course the Queen

Defending a no-trump
contract what card would you
lead holding this hand?

Holding this hand you should
lead the Q

On the lead of the 6♦
from this hand your
partner would calculate
the Rule of Eleven and
with say two cards higher
than the 6 in hand and say
two cards higher than the 6
now shown in dummy,
your partner would know
there is only one card

above the 6 in the hidden hand. The Declarer would do the same
exercise. Once that higher card has been played from the hidden
hand, then that hand will be void of a card in the lead suit above the
six. The problem, at least with me, is remembering that fact.

Still on the subject of what to lead against a no-trump contract.....

Leading a 10.

Not usually recognised as an opening lead against a no-trump contract but I find the following lead very useful. When I have led a 10 of any suit, my partner immediately knows that I have two honours left in my hand. Look how the cards are distributed in the following hand.

```
        Q85
         N
AJ103  W     E  K92
         S
        764
```

The 10 is led by West and Declarer plays the 5 from Dummy. East does not need to play the K because there cannot be a card above the 10 in South's hand. Seeing the Queen in North's hand, East knows that partner holds the Ace and the Jack and plays the 2.

Look at another example of leading a 10.

West leads the 10 and after the Dummy hand goes on the table, East knows that South will hold only one honour in the suit led and if South takes the trick with the Jack then East will know for sure the location of the AK.

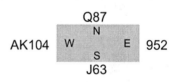

```
        Q87
         N
AK104  W     E  952
         S
        J63
```

Perhaps the opposition could just not agree find a suit.

Consider how the auction went. Often there is a bit of a bidding argument. For example – one side bids Hearts, the other Spades, then back to Hearts and then Spades. The opposition simply cannot agree on a suit and with a bit of a huff and a puff one of the opposition pair reluctantly bids 3nt. I say reluctantly because very often the body language tells all. Consider leading the suit that was bid by the Declarer's partner, to become the Dummy, especially if you are short of that suit yourself because it is likely your partner will have some interesting stops in the suit.

The Fourth Suit
Did the opposition resort to a <u>fourth suit forcing bid</u> (discussed in chapter 12) to reach their no-trump contract? Having bid 3 suits, the bid of the fourth suit is normally an exercise in finding cover in that suit with a no-trump contract in mind. Normally that suit will be the weakest in the two opposing hands and could well be a good suit to lead. Even if the fourth suit was not bid, that suit is generally a good suit to lead. After all, they've bid three suits between them so you and your partner could well have some winners in the fourth suit. Just a thought.

Use your imagination.
As you sit there wondering what to lead from those 13 cards in your hand, have a thought as to what suit and what card the Declarer would like you to lead. Imagine you have shown your hand of cards to the Declarer.

What suit and then what card would the Declarer choose?

The Psyche Bid
It was years after I first learnt Bridge that I considered I understood the Psyche bid. My understanding is that when you deliberately make a bid ………… hold on a second an interruption and I will explain the reason for the distraction. Perhaps a Psyche distraction. Last night we arrived home late and when I undressed my shirt came away from me in the same action of removing my jumper and the two garments still joined together as if still on my back were placed on the chair. Not my usual practice I hasten to add, but late last night I did not bother to do an uncoupling. This morning when dressing in my very comfortable tatty garments which I wear round the house, including 'those trousers' the two joined up garments remained on the chair.

The interruption in my endeavour to explain the Psyche bid was, as you can guess, Margaret enquiring why the two garments were still very good friends, my words not hers, and that she did not like shirt buttons done up when shirts needed washing. Obviously the

50

shirt did not need washing because it is now hanging neatly on the back of the bedroom chair ready for me to wear this evening. The shirt had only been worn for three hours last night and it was my plan to wear the same shirt and jumper for the same time this evening when the dressing would have been relatively easy. Anyway enough of that – back to the Psyche bid.

The Psyche bid is a conscious attempt to fool the opposition in believing you have strength, cards or suits when no such strength, cards or suits are present. Not illegal mind you, provided the bid contains the same element of surprise for the psycher's partner as it does for the opponents. Not recommended unless you have kamikaze tendencies or a very understanding partner.

Now perhaps psyche over-crowding.
My Father and I plus eight other travelling companions all used to board the train at Chesham, a terminus station, in Buckinghamshire and travel to Baker Street in London in the single slam door compartment carriage which had five seats aside and fairly comfortable seats at that. We all used to travel in the same compartment each morning and on particularly cold mornings the windows remained shut so that by the time the train had reached Harrow on the Hill, some 20 or so miles away, we had developed a lovely 'fug up'. The air was stale but we were all comfortable and warm. Then some person or persons would join the train for a standing position and invariably one of the two windows would be opened without reference to the regulars and out would go the 'lovely fug' and in would come the cold fresh air which developed into a penetrating draught when the train started to move.

The remedy was clear. We needed to dissuade others joining our compartment. On many occasions, as the train pulled into Harrow on the hill, those sitting on the off side of the platform would stand and crowd the platform doorway to give the impression to those passengers on the platform that the compartment was already full to capacity and it worked a treat. When the train started off we all settled back into our seats in comfort and the 'fug up' would be maintained until we reached Finchley Road.

Defending and Playing a No-trump Contract

You've opened 1nt or you've responded to partner's 1nt opening and so forth. You have also discovered what card to lead against a no-trump contract by the opposition. Now we'll have a look at what happens when the 1nt contract is played from two different aspects:

- as a Defender and then
- as a Declarer

My card play is often weak through carelessness and thoughtlessness and often I do not see the obvious and as such I will not be delving deeply into the whys and wherefores of playing the cards. What I will do is just give you a few pointers on the lead and some thoughts on some aspects of play.

You are Defending a No-Trump Contract.

a). **Unblocking**. Your partner has led from a long suit and if an honour card then it is the top of an internal high sequence or the top of a high sequence. If you hold a high honour card yourself as shown in this set of hands, then consider a possible problem you may cause your partner by not playing your high card to unblock.

South opened 1nt. West passes needing 10 points to overcall the Spades at 2 level. North is balanced and holding 13 points innocently bids 3nt.

South is Declarer in a 3nt contract and West is on lead. After drawing the Q♠ from hand, holding it face down and enquiring as to any questions of partner, the card is placed on the table and the North hand goes down as Dummy for all to see. The 7 is played from Dummy and now what card should East play? The 8 or overtake with the King.

	N	♠	76
		♥	QJ8
		♦	K8432
		♣	AK5

W					E		
♠	AQJ95				♠	K8
♥	107		Dealer		♥	5432
♦	975		South		♦	J6
♣	Q102				♣	87643

	S	♠	10432
		♥	AK96
		♦	AQ10
		♣	J9

If East takes the view that the King will later make a trick and plays the 8, that could lessen the chances of West capitalising on that good lead. If East now plays the 8 then the King will be left in hand and will win the next round of Spades unless West overtakes with the Ace which will then destroy West's ability to defeat the contract. A difficult decision to make, I know, but in the example East must overtake West's Queen with the King and lead back the 8 when West will make four more tricks and defeat the contract. East must play the King to <u>unblock</u>.

b). Your partner has selected one card from thirteen cards to lead against a no-trump contract. Why has that card been selected? There will normally be a reason and <u>unless the cards in Dummy dictate otherwise</u> that suit should invariably be played again as soon as possible. Even though there are two certain winners in Dummy say the Ace and King, lead that suit with a view to getting rid of them because your partner will want them out of the way as soon as possible.

c). Hold on to an Ace if you spot the Declarer trying to set up a suit in the Dummy hand with no other entries. Look at this example:

South is Declarer in a no-trump contract and will lead the suit with the hope of drawing the opposition Ace and will be very frustrated when the Ace does not appear after the second round. South will 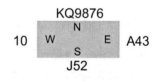 be particularly annoyed if the North hand does not have any other winners in other suits to reach those remaining winners once the Ace has fallen. If East takes the Ace winner at round one or two of that suit then Declarer will be able to get across the table into Dummy's hand for the remaining winners. By ducking the first two rounds, East will thwart South's plans and I can tell you from bitter experience that it is never comfortable to have been thwarted.

d). If your partner has bid a suit during the auction then it is a good idea to lead that suit through Declarer to partner provided, of course, the cards in the tabled Dummy hand do not dictate otherwise. The Declarer will have stops in your partner's bid suit but it will be uncomfortable to have that suit led when the opposition player who bid the suit is sitting behind.

e). Remember the suit your partner led because there may be several rounds of other suits before you have the chance to lead the suit again. Be careful not to discard the last card of the suit your partner wants led.

You are the Declarer in a No-Trump contract.
No need to remind you that the opposition will be doing their level best to defeat the contract and therefore be careful not to assist them in their plans. Here are a few pointers:

a). When the Dummy hand goes on the table count your certain winners and when doing so do not count more tricks than the number of cards in your longest holding. Consider how those winners are to be cashed. A silly example but there are only five tricks in these two hands.

AKQJ10

9876

b). Before cashing certain winners, it is important that you <u>establish winners in other suits first</u>. I'll say again. Before you cash your certain top winners which are going to make tricks in any event, <u>establish winners in other suits first.</u> If top cards in the suits in which you need to make winners are in opposition hands then try and get those top cards out before leading off your certain winners.

c). If the defenders bid a suit during the auction then the likely whereabouts of some high cards in that suit are known. Also do some counting. You know how many points there are in your hand and the Dummy hand on the table. If one of the Defenders opened the bidding then you can assume at least 12 points are in that hand and if the Defender overcalled then assume about 10 points. You should be able to have a fairly good guess as to the number of points held by the other Defender.

d). **Ducking** and **Hold-up Play.** You do not have to win a trick just because you have the top card in the suit. In your endeavour to establish tricks where higher cards are in enemy hands you should 'duck' one or two rounds as demonstrated in this hand.

You are the Declarer at South and you want to establish a suit because of the length in the Dummy hand. Assume you have no winners in the Dummy hand other than the Ace. The suit will not be led by the Defenders for obvious reasons so you will need to do the leading yourself. At the

```
                A98643
              N
        Q2  W       E  K10
              S
                J75
```

first opportunity lead the 5 and play low in Dummy. Four cards gone, two left in enemy hands and you will hope for an even split when leading that suit again. Looking at the distribution of the above hand it is now safe to play the Ace but in reality those two missing cards could be held in one hand so on the second round of that suit you should still play low and then cash the remaining winners in Dummy with the Ace when next you are on lead.

What you will have achieved is four winning tricks in that example just shown having let the Defenders win the first two tricks. On the distribution of the above hand you would have drawn the Defender's cards on the second round by taking the Ace but could you be sure the distribution was 2/2 rather than 3/1? Always best to be safe than sorry because the defenders will know exactly what you are about and will endeavour to stop your little plan.

It's called <u>Hold-Up Play.</u>

A8643	opposite	975	Duck two rounds - play Ace on third hopefully making three tricks in that suit.
AK9532	opposite	87	Duck first round then play Ace and King hopefully making 5 tricks in that suit
Q87543	opposite	962	Duck first 2 rounds- play to Q on third hopefully making 4 tricks in that suit.

e). If there is a long suit in either your hand as Declarer or the Dummy hand without any worthwhile honours then lead that suit whenever possible in order to remove the opposition honours but do this before you cash all the winners in other suits. Look at this example.

You are South and trying to achieve 3nt. You will welcome the opposition leading the suit in order to assist you in setting up winners in the North Dummy hand. Once they see the tabled Dummy hand you will not get any assistance in that suit from the opposition; you will have to do all the work yourself. If you need tricks from the suit to achieve your contract then you will have to start working on the suit as soon as possible. Each time you win a trick, lead the suit you are trying to establish. At the first opportunity lead the 10 and then at the next opportunity lead the 2. As there are five missing cards, it may take three rounds to remove the AKQ from enemy hands do the job hence the necessity to keep a winner in another suit in Dummy for you to attain entry across the table. Bear in mind that the opposition will do all they can to remove that outside entry before you have the opportunity of cashing the remaining winners.

f). Do not win the first trick and then lead the opposition suit back to them unless it is to your advantage having seen your partner's Dummy hand.

g). You're playing a no-trump contract and West, not necessarily the first lead, leads the 6. What will you play?

Do you play the Q which may be beaten or do you play low? Play low because to win the trick East will have to play the Ace or the King in which case you will subsequently win one trick in that suit. Play the Queen at the outset, it will very likely be taken by the Ace or the King and then the Jack stands little chance of success.

h). If you are somewhat worried about a particular suit which has not been led then you can try a little bit of cunning. Suppose you have six cards between the two hands, say 3/3, with no chance of winning a trick and fear that suit being led by the opposition. Consider leading the suit yourself and the opposition, if they are not too smart, may not return that suit straight away for fear of assisting you setting up winners, which is something they will wish to avoid.

i). Finding that one of the Defenders can make additional tricks after the suit has been exhausted from all other hands, then be mindful of that player winning a trick and making those winners. Make the other opponent win the trick rather than the 'dangerous' player.

j). When the opposition lead a suit and you have the choice of winning in Dummy or in hand then with a suit that needs establishing in the Dummy hand for example, would it not be better to retain that entry into Dummy and win the trick in hand? This is most important when the hand which contains the suit which needs establishing is short of entries through other suits. Look at this example. Plan your play carefully to avoid ending up not being unable to reach winners and I'm sure you do not need reminding that the opposition will do all they can to stop you reaching winners.

	N	♠	K85			
		♥	AKQ			
		♦	J43			
W		♣	J764			
♠	J102			♠	Q7643	
♥	10987	Dealer		♥	J5	
♦	A76	West		♦	102	
♣	A103			♣	K852	E
	♠	A9				
	♥	6432				
	♦	KQ985				
	♣	Q9	S			

North ends up playing a 3nt contract and East leads the 4♠.

Declarer is relaxed about the lead having the Ace in Dummy and the King in hand. Declarer takes the trick with the Ace (bad move) and then ducks when the suit is led again and then takes the third round of Spades with the King. In between Declarer plans to remove the A♦ from enemy hands to establish the Diamonds.

Pretty good plan eh! Yes, a very good plan but it will only work if the Defenders are not thinking properly.

Just look what happens after the A♠ is played on the first round. Declarer (North), with the J♦ in hand to play, then leads a low Diamond from Dummy with the idea of extracting the Ace from the Defenders but they do not play ball – West ducks. West also ducks the second round and takes the trick on the third round with the Ace.

Do you see what has happened? Having made a huge mistake at the outset and <u>not planned the play and taken the first trick in the wrong hand,</u> the Declarer, by playing the A♠ from Dummy instead of the K♠ from hand, removed the only certain entry into Dummy before establishing the Diamonds. As West held up playing the A♦, the Declarer can now not reach the remaining Diamond winners in Dummy unless of course, the Defenders allow the Q♣ to win a trick, which they most definitely will not.   There's more………….

Not only do the Defenders upset the Declarer's plans by not playing the A♦ straight away, when the Ace does win a trick, West will have remembered partner's opening Spade lead. If North does not duck the second round of Spades but wins with the K♠, then when West gets in again with the A♣ the third Spade in hand will be despatched across to East's winners. All because North did not think to duck the first round of Spades.

It only needs a little thought at the outset. After the first card is played the Declarer should do four things:

- Count the certain tricks in each suit
- Calculate the additional tricks needed.
- Consider the suits where the extra tricks will be found.
- Try and establish the suits for the extra tricks as soon as possible. Do not take the certain tricks first.

k). And finally an end to this long winded session on no-trumps. Don't forget though – when Declarer, never show disappointment at your partner's Dummy hand when it goes onto the table. It is possible that the opposition may find comfort in your dissatisfaction and you certainly do not want the opposition to be in a state of comfort about anything.

In case I forget - Some forgetfulness whilst playing Bridge.
Recently, it seems, every time I play Bridge I do something silly and
kick myself for being so stupid and then I feel better when other folk
do the same thing. If I only gave my playing a little more thought I
would not have so many mental bruises. In my earlier years I was
called Mr Quick 'person' and person was not the word they actually
used. If only I gave situations a little more thought I would achieve
better results be it Bridge or anything else for that matter.

Take the other evening. I was defending a 3nt contract and I had
three cards left in my hand. The Q♦, the 4♦ and the J♣. On two
rounds earlier the Declarer ruffed my Ace of Clubs but two rounds
later could I remember that ruff? Could I heck? I forgot and instead
of discarding that then useless J♣ I threw away the low Diamond
and had to play the Queen on Declarer's Ace and guess what won
Declarer's ninth trick - a low Diamond. That error was expensive
earning us a very decisive bottom.

I do have an excuse – I am fast reaching…. No. I have reached that
age where the likelihood of being forgetful is strong but what does
worry me is that an incident just a minute earlier, possibly less,
should be forgotten and I'm not surprised that Ingrid across the way
gave me a look that I can only describe as menacing. I was not too
worried however because she was relying on me for a lift home.

Had it not been for a comment by the opposition after another
game had finished and I was marking the result on the traveller with
some despondency, Ingrid would not have realised another Stephens
boo-boo which makes me wonder, every time I think about it,
whether I should still be playing Bridge. Fortunately Ingrid is a very
good natured lady and after my apology she dismissed the oversight
with a wave of her left hand as just one of those things.

Just one of those things be blowed. I had been the Declarer sitting
North in a 3nt contract. The hand had been played several times and
the traveller (the score sheet) was awash with 3nt contracts making
10 tricks and North/South scores of 630. Entering the East/West
score of 100 my having achieved only 8 tricks and wondering what

had gone wrong, the charming lady on my left kindly mentioned that she had called a Spade in the bidding and had quite expected me to finesse the Queen in Dummy.

Of course she would have expected me to guess where the King was sitting but I can't be expected to think about that when I'm in the middle of building a shed in the garden. Yes, I'm in the throws of building a shed and so far it looks pretty good in spite Ruth, my long standing Bridge partner from Hurstpierpoint, thinking it's all very sad and suggested that I should have had a brain implant rather than a tooth implant I had recently. She was joking. Of course she was.

Seriously though, I am conscious of forgetfulness and wonder whether it is the start of things to come. Of late, there have been several occasions when I have not been able to remember whether or not the Ace has been played and then find my King snapped up by the opposition. What with the memory and the inability to count to 13 sometimes and finding a loose opposition trump card being played, I'm wondering whether I should actually be playing Bridge at all. I seem to be having more and more 'senior moments'.

I have reached that stage in life when I feel I have an excuse for an occasional memory lapse but I did feel ancient the other day following a barbeque at my Daughter's house when football on the back patch of grass ensued. Three ladies sat down as spectators and I was summoned to be the goalie by several voices obviously very mindful that I was of an age where running around kicking a football was considered too risky. I was the goalkeeper and let me tell you that I may as well have been a spectator for all the good I did but I was able to blame a crab apple tree three yards in front of the goal for several misses due to not knowing from which side of the tree the ball would be shot and the width of the goal I was supposed to be defending, compared with the width of the opposing goal, led me to believe I was at a distinct disadvantage. For the time being I will stick to Bridge.

Your partner has bid 1nt
Then your RHO Doubles
or your LHO Doubles after your pass.

The Double will normally be a Penalty Double and the Doubler will have a strong hand and defeat in mind.

I will be discussing Doubles later on but whilst on the subject of no-trumps I will explain what action, if any, should be taken after the opposition Double your partner's 1nt opening bid.

Your partner opens 1nt and the opposition Double which normally means a strong hand with between 15-18 points. After a 1nt bid the Double is a <u>Penalty Double</u> which means the Doubler has high hopes of defeating the 1nt contract. Both the opener's partner and the doubler's partner must consider the implications of the Double in the light of points held in their hands. The lower the number of points the more urgent is the action to be taken to rescue which should be considered holding less than 7 points. A rescue bid will be either a suit or a conventional bid which bid will ask partner to say something.

Remember

If your partner's 1nt bid is Doubled and neither you nor the Doubler's partner take action – your partner will not bid again and the Double will stand which will be fine if you have enough points to withstand the threat.

Unopposed bidding after 1nt opening

1nt – 2nt	a). showing 11/12 points and no interest in a four card major. Transfers not agreed or b). Transfers agreed and showing exactly 12 pts.
1nt – 2c	Stayman if agreed otherwise 2c is a weak take-out.
1nt – 2d	a). Weak take-out. Transfers not used or b). Transfer bid into Hearts.
1nt – 2h	a). Weak take-out. Transfers not used or b). Transfer into Spades.
1nt-2c-2h-3c	Weak but length in Clubs & bidding Stayman first.
1nt-2c-2d-pass	Length in Diamonds and bidding Stayman first.
1nt-2d-2h-2nt	Transfers used showing 5 Hearts and 11/12 points
1nt-2h-2s-3nt	Transfers used showing 5 Spades and 13 (+) points
1nt-2h-2s-pass	Weak take-out into Spades using transfers.
1nt-2d-2h-pass	Weak take-out into Hearts using Transfers.
1nt – 2s	Weak take-out into Spades not using Transfers
1nt – 2s	Showing exactly 11 points using Transfers.
1nt – 3nt	Showing 13/18 points and balanced
1nt-2c-2h-2nt	Showing 4 Spades and 11/12 points.
1nt-2c-2h-3nt	Showing 4 Spades and game points.
1nt-2c-2s-4s	Showing at least four Spades and game points

ARE YOU GUILTY OF THESE OFFENCES?	It is a Bridge rule that until a lead is made to the next trick, the Declarer or both Defenders may re-examine their own defaced card. They may not examine cards of a previous trick. Any player who has not yet turned over their card thus hiding its

face can ask that all cards just played be shown. **However once a player's own card has been turned over and defaced then the right to see the cards of the Defenders is withdrawn.**

I do smile to myself at a very common practice as seen in many clubs. A player has already defaced the played card and then wishes to see the cards of the other players, including the Dummy. The common practice, quite illegal, is for the player to pick up and face own card without even glancing at it, knowing full well what card it was and ask for the other cards to be seen and invariably everybody obliges without a murmur.

But the funny part is that the player will never want to review his or her own card which has been turned over and laid to rest but nevertheless the player fully faces or half faces own card with a quick flip without looking at it as if the card had never been defaced in the first place. The Declarer never wants to view own card but would never dream of asking others to turn their cards with their own card being left unfaced because that is against the rules. It is as if the turn of their defaced card makes everything alright.

On the same subject there's something else I have noticed. If a player asks a specific player to face their defaced card, you will find that inevitably everybody at the table including Dummy will deface their cards.

And another thing already mentioned,
when playing with bidding boxes,
all bids <u>must stay on the table</u> until the first card is led.

Are you guilty?

The importance of ducking either as a Declarer or Defender in order to achieve a subsequent advantage.

When Declarer in a no-trump contract and you hold, for example, Axx in hand and the Dummy hand has xxx and that suit is led then you should duck the first two rounds and win the A on the third round by which time the RHO is likely to be void of the suit and thus unable to lead the suit to LHO winners.	When in opposition defending a no-trump contract and you hold Axx for example, it may be to your advantage to consider ducking the first two rounds of the suit when it is seen that the Declarer is trying to establish a long suit in Dummy and there are no other winners in Dummy enabling Declarer to reach the remaining winners. There will be occasions when your Ace is not actually played but you have in fact stopped the Declarer making additional tricks.

The Ace of course; so why do what the opposition want you to do?

If you are the Declarer and the contract is no-trumps and you have Axx in hand and xxx in Dummy and your LHO leads that suit, what will the Defender want you to play? **The Ace of course; so why do what the opposition want you to do?**	If you are one of the Defenders in a no-trump contract and you hold Axx and the Declarer leads that suit and you believe the Declarer has intentions of establishing that suit then what card will the Declarer want you to play? **The Ace of course; so why do what the opposition want you to do?**

The hold-up card does not have to be the Ace but if a King then be careful you do not delay the play of that card to your detriment. Don't get yourself in a position where the opposition Ace will take your previously held-up King.

Farmhouse B & B
Sipping coffee, a holiday brochure has caught my eye and in particular a block headed Farmhouse B & B.

What's the difference? Farmhouse B & B and just B & B? As it happens I do know what B & B means. Bed and Breakfast rather than Brainless and Boring. Presumably the accommodation in Farmhouse B & B is within a farmhouse building complex and probably a converted cow shed, with a bedroom, a bathroom and a loo and full English breakfast just as one would get in any other B & B accommodation. If the accommodation was within a laundry then presumably the sign would read laundry B & B and if part of an Indian take-away the sign would read Indian take-away B & B. Goes without saying.

I have an idea the B&B people who own the farmhouse consider their accommodation more attractive because it is within a farm complex which conjures up in the minds of customers, freshly baked bread, warm milk straight from the cow and eggs with deep orange yokes. The fact that three cockerels crow from 4 am each morning which start the four dogs barking and that dreadful smell of the silage or pig manure is of little consequence. The eggs at breakfast come from the farm battery house situated behind the cowshed whereas behind the laundry B & B is a large field where the chickens are happily roaming about pecking grubs all day long.

What is a Farm Shop? It is a shop in a country district, surrounded by lovely fields with sheep grazing and the corn swaying back and forth in the breeze. The person in charge of the shop or the buyer will be seen at the fruit and veg. market each morning with all the other buyers who have their retail outlets in the town who will sell their produce at just a little less than the selling price in the farm shop.

Fresher? – of course the fruit and vegetables will be fresher in the farm shop; what else would you expect?

Now five sample sets of hands with no-trumps in mind.

Hand Set 1.

Opening bid is 1nt by West.
Partner bids Stayman but does not get the reply sought.
Contract 4s by West – Spades mentioned by implication.

	N		
		♠	J102
		♥	Q62
		♦	KJ1087
W		♣	108

♠	KQ96		♠	A875
♥	A973	Dealer	♥	1085
♦	94	West	♦	AQ6
♣	A52		♣	K43

	♠	43	E
	♥	KJ4	
	♦	532	
	♣	QJ976	S

The Bidding.
N/Sth pass throughout.
West – opens 1nt
East bids 2c (Stayman)
West replies – 2h
East bids – stop 3nt
West bids – 4s.

West opens 1nt with 12-14 points in hand and balanced, although the Diamond suit looks a bit suspect.

East immediately knows that game is a good possibility holding 13 points and with four Spades in hand, sets about enquiring whether another set of four Spades exists in partner's hand by bidding 2c (Stayman).

West, after announcing 'Stayman', will bid 2h, holding 4 cards in both majors. Not satisfied with the reply, holding only 3 Heart cards, East will now bid to game, holding those 13 points - stop 3nt obviously not knowing that there are four Spade cards as well in the hand opposite, but aware of the possibility.

East has now given West some very positive information based on the possibility of West only holding 12 points and four Heart cards. First of all East has bid to game so must hold 13 or more points and secondly East must have four Spades in hand. Why? East bid Stayman. To bid the conventional 2c, East would have had at least 11 points and at least one four card major in order to escape should the answer not be satisfactory. Having bid 3nt after West's Heart reply to Stayman, it is obvious that Hearts were of no interest, so East must hold four Spades and have 13 or more points.

Holding two four card majors, West correctly replied 2h to partner's Stayman enquiry. Following East's 3nt bid, West is now very much aware of the fact that there are four Spades and 13 or more points opposite and with some confidence will bid to game in Spades – 4s.

The Play - It always used to be good practice, when defending a suit contract, to lead the top of a doubleton, and the subsequent play of a lower card would indicate a shortage, called Petering, but today the practice is not so popular because the play does notify the opposition and the less the opposition know about your hand, the better. However North, who is on lead in this set of hands, does not have much choice in the matter. Not wanting to lead trumps or Hearts where four cards of the suit are sitting in West's hand, North is left with either a Diamond or a Club lead. As West bid 1nt then there is a good chance that the Diamond honours in hand and positioned behind West, will be very useful in defence so North is left with Clubs and in spite of what I said above about what is not considered good practice today, North should lead the 10♣

When East's Dummy hand goes down onto the table, North will be pleased that a Diamond was not led and it is the Diamond suit upon which West will concentrate upon too.

Declarer will now plan the play and note with some regret that there are 4 losers in the two hands. There are no Spade losers, but two Heart losers, one Diamond loser and one Club loser which will mean that the contract will fail unless one of the losers is taken care of, so to speak. The obvious suit is the Diamonds with the Ace and Queen sitting in East's hand opposite. The best chance of making the contract will be for Declarer to lead a Diamond through North in the hope of winning the Queen, with the King still sitting in North's hand. In other words Declarer will need to try and finesse (make a trick with a lower card) with the Q♦ which, in this case, will be successful and the contract will be made.

<u>Hand Set 2.</u>

This is a situation where your partner has opened 1nt and you are most unsuitable for no-trumps having a very unbalanced hand but your longest suit is Clubs and they are significant. On these hands it is immaterial whether Transfers have been agreed or not but the Stayman convention has been agreed. East/West pass throughout.

	N				
	♠	void			
	♥	973			
	♦	9753			
W	♣	AQ9876			
♠ A7642				♠	9853
♥ Q84		Dealer		♥	A105
♦ K86		South		♦	AJ10
♣ 43				♣	K105
	♠	KQJ10		E	
	♥	KJ62			
	♦	Q42			
	♣	J2	S		

<u>The Bidding</u>
South – 1nt
North – 2c (Stayman)
South bids – 2h
North bids 3c.
All then pass.

South opens the bidding with 12/14 and a balanced hand.

West passes. North is obviously not suitable for no-trumps and with less than 11 points must take partner out of no-trumps. North has two choices. Leave things as they are and hope that partner has cover in the Spades, Hearts and Diamonds or bid 2c and take little notice of partner's reply and then bid 3c knowing that partner must have at least two Club cards to open 1nt.

Holding North's hand the choice is easy. Very unbalanced and with that void and Clubs of good quality and quantity North will bid 2c (Stayman). South will announce Stayman and will bid the lower of the two four card majors – 2h. North will bid 3c. South will pass realising the weak hand and intentions opposite.

One could argue that having a strong holding of Clubs or any other suit for that matter, could be an advantage in that partner may have cover in the other suits and a 1nt contract making say 9 tricks (150) is better than a 3c contract making 10 tricks (130). It's the chance you take and vulnerability will come into the equation.

The Stayman convention is not only a vehicle for asking for a four card major, the convention can also be used as a weak take-out into Clubs or Diamonds as described earlier.

Having no lead indications from partner, East prefers not to lead a trump or a suit where the Ace or King is held so with Hobson's choice will lead the 8♠ which will indicate that an honour is not held. If you and your partner have agreed not to lead away from an Ace or a King unless partner has bid the suit then the lead of a low card will indicate that a Queen or Jack is held. If you lead a high non honour then that will indicate an honour is not held.

When 'on lead' although you will have 13 cards from which to choose one card to lead, often you are left with Hobson Choice and have to select the best of the bunch and the one you will choose is the card of the suit in your opinion will most likely create an advantage for your side later in the play.

****

To my knowledge Thomas Hobson, known as the Cambridge Carrier never played Bridge. He is best known as the name behind the expression **Hobson's Choice** and do please excuse me if all this irrelevant information is to you 'old hat'. To me it's not. He was a carrier who delivered mail between London and Cambridge operating a livery stable outside the gates of St Catherine's College. When not needed, Hobson's horses were rented out to students and academic staff of the university.

It was not long before Hobson discovered that his fastest horses were the most popular and to prevent his best horses being overworked and becoming exhausted he developed a system whereby his horses were rented out by strict rotation and his customers had to have the horse nearest the stable door or none at all. Hence no choice at all and that's the problem sometimes when you have to decide what to lead.

Don't forget, if you lead an honour card, an A, K, Q or J, unless it is your partner's suit bid during the auction, you are generally guaranteeing the card below.

Hand Set 3.

You've game points and 5 card major. Partner opens 1nt and you reply giving your partner the choice of game in either your suit or in no-trumps. Stayman agreed.

East and West pass throughout.

N	♠	A54
	♥	KQ103
	♦	Q10
W	♣	K762

♠	Q862			♠	10
♥	J76	Dealer		♥	A852
♦	AJ5	North		♦	7632
♣	954			♣	J1083

	♠	KJ973	E
	♥	94	
	♦	K984	
	♣	AQ	S

The Bidding not using transfers

North opens 1nt. An unbalanced South has 13 points and knows that game is a very good possibility even if there are only 12 points opposite. South will invite game and confirm the five Spades straight away by bidding – stop 3s. That is a forcing bid which demands another bid from partner – either 3nt or 4s. North having 3 Spade cards and knowing there a 5 Spades opposite will bid 4s. By not using Transfers South becomes the Declarer.

West leads 6♥ or 5♣. A nondescript lead but what else is there to do?

The Bidding using Transfers.

An alternative method for South, as Transfers have been agreed is for South to respond to North's 1nt bid by bidding 2h, requesting a transfer to Spades. After North bids the requested 2s, South would then bid – stop 3nt confirming not only five Spades are held but game points as well and then North would make the decision as to 3nt or game in Spades. Holding 3 Spade cards North bids to game in Spades – 4s. By using Transfers the Declarer is now North.

East, with a better choice of lead which will be the 3♣ to confirm the honour held which turns out to be of no consequence.

Hand Set 4. – So often it is the lead that defeats the contract.

The East/West partnership has reached 3nt in the bidding and looking at their hands one wonders what can possibly go wrong. East is the Declarer having opened 1nt and is in fact quite relaxed about South's lead of the 5♣ and when West's Dummy hand goes on the table East seems not to have a care in the world. 1 Spade loser, 1 Heart loser, no Diamond losers and at the most only two Club losers. In East's mind the contract is made.

	N					
		♠	9754			
		♥	K93			
		♦	10543			
W		♣	A2			
♠	KJ			♠	Q862	
♥	QJ2		Dealer	♥	A854	
♦	AK9862		East	♦	QJ	
♣	108			♣	KJ9	
		♠	A103			E
		♥	1076			
		♦	7			
		♣	Q76543	S		

The Bidding
East opens 1nt.
South/North pass throughout.
West bids 3d.   East bids 3nt

West has a long Diamond suit and 14 points. Game is likely but West must show those Diamonds and bids - stop 3d, which is comforting for East who bids 3nt.

South is on lead and this example will show just how important it is to lead from a long suit when defending a no-trump contract. In this example if South leads a low Club then the contract will fail. The failure of the contract is caused by getting two early rounds of Clubs and having that vital A♠ entry.

North will win the trick with the Ace and immediately lead back the other Club and it matters not whether East plays the King or the Jack because South will retain three Club winners which will be cashed when Spades are led. If North does not carelessly throw away Diamonds it looks as though the contract will fail by 2 tricks.

Little did South realise when sorting the cards at the outset that those lowly Clubs would defeat the contract. Had South not lead a Club at the outset and had spent the Ace of Spades before the Clubs had been led, the contract would likely not have been defeated.

Hand Set 5.

Having game points and six Hearts, North knows that partner must have at least 2 Heart cards to have opened 1nt therefore a fit in Hearts. Holding the singleton Diamond, I would take the bull by the horns and bid stop 4h straight away without giving partner the choice of 3nt or 4h as would be the case with a 3h reply.

If Transfers had been agreed then North would bid 2d, South would reply 2h and North would bid 4h.

	N	♠	KJ
		♥	AJ9763
		♦	K
W		♣	Q972

♠	432		♠	A1086
♥	Q8	Dealer	♥	542
♦	A9843	South	♦	1062
♣	853		♣	K106

			E
♠	Q975		
♥	K10		
♦	QJ75		
♣	AJ4	S	

The Bidding
South opens 1nt. West passes
North bids stop 4h
Then all pass

North knows all the answers and does not need to invite partner or ask partner. North knows there are 12-14 points and at least two Hearts opposite. With game points and six reasonable looking Hearts in hand, North bids straight to game. No mucking about.

Without transfers, North would be the Declarer and I reckon East would lead the 6♦ and follow with the 10 if the suit was led again. Using Transfers, South would be the Declarer in which case West would probably lead the 5♣ and then play the 8 on the second round.

CHAPTER 	Opening Bidding at the 1 level and the Responses holding less than 11 points

If you have a hand holding between 10 - 19 points and not a 12-14 point balanced hand upon which you would open 1nt (the weak no-trump) you will open at the 1 level in a suit. 1c, 1d, 1h or 1s.

Without either a six card suit or two five card suits, when you can add two distributional points to a 10/11 point hand to open the bidding or you qualify under the Rule of 20 explained next, you must have at least 12 HCP's to open at the 1 level and all Bridge players remember **Length before Strength**	As you would expect by now there is the inevitable exception and this is when you have a longish suit and can see 8 playing tricks in your hand when you can open the bidding at the 2 level with less than 20 points This will be discussed later.

The Rule of 20 - Latterly in *The Road Across the Bridge* I mentioned the Rule of 19/20. I mentioned both numbers because when I learnt to play it was the Rule of 19 but it seems with inflation it is now known as the Rule of 20. If you have cards in two suits, split 5/4 then add the number of cards you have in the two long suits to the number of HCP's in your hand and if the addition reaches 20 then open the bidding at the 1 level in the five card suit but think again if your two long suits are a bit ropey like this hand.

♠ A5
♥ KJ
♦ J6342
♣ Q842

The total still reaches 20 when you add cards in the two longest suits to the HCP's but just look at the poor quality of the two long suits. When the longest suits are like those as shown then, in my opinion, best you do not open the bidding 1d. Just pass

♠	J7
♥	AQ842
♦	KJ53
♣	95

Now look at this example: There are 11 HCP and 9 cards in the two long suits. Adding the 9 cards to the HCP's the sum is 20, so holding this hand you could open the bidding 1h holding only 11 points.

Normally with only 10/11 points you would open with either a six card suit or 2x5 card suits. If your partner supports your Hearts by bidding 2h then that is one up-shut up and you pass. If your partner bids 1s then you would bid 2d which would confirm holding four Diamonds and Five Hearts.

Baring the exceptions you will open the bidding at the 1 level holding 12-19 points.

Length before Strength
Quantity before Quality

If you have two five card suits you open the higher sequence suit but if the suits are both black then open the Club suit first because it is easier to introduce the Spade suit later at the one level if your partner responds 1d or 1h. Same with two four card black suits.

If you have two four card suits and both biddable then open the higher suit first except when they are both majors. Holding 4 Hearts and 4 Spades open the Hearts first because if you open the Spades and then rebid Hearts you will confirm you hold 5 Spade cards.

If you have a Roman hand – 4441 – and the four card suits are all biddable then if the singleton is red, open suit below and if the singleton is a black card then open a Heart.

If singleton is a Spade open 1h
If singleton is a Heart open 1d
If singleton is a Diamond open 1c
If singleton is a Club open 1h.

If one of the three four card suits is not biddable
then treat as a two suiter.

74

Always bear in mind that if your partner bids <u>another suit</u> after you have opened at the 1 level you are obliged, in fact, your partner expects you to bid again. The emphasis is upon partner bidding <u>another suit</u> because if your partner bids 1nt after your suit opening then you are <u>not</u> obliged to bid again.

Your opening bid tells your partner about the 10-19 points in your hand but your rebid, after your partner's response, will confirm not only a narrower window of points but also whether your opening hand was weak or strong. With this in mind, you must be careful not to open the bidding in a suit when you should have opened 1nt because your rebid could be difficult and remember a rebid of your opening suit or bidding another suit at the 2 level will usually confirm 5 cards in your first bid suit.

I will comment later on weak, strong and very strong opening hands but for the moment just take note that after an opening bid at the 1 level in a suit, you will not make a jump bid on your rebid unless you have more than 14 points. The mention of **Stop** before the bid normally indicates a jump bid.

What's all this Stop business? I hear you saying. In a nutshell, you say **Stop** before a jump bid just to give your LHO, who was not expecting the jump, another 10 seconds of thinking time because too much hesitation in Bridge is a 'crime'.

Hearts are stronger, but <u>length before strength</u>. It is quantity rather than quality you must consider. On this hand you would open 1s and then bid the Hearts next confirming a 5 Spade holding.

♠	K8754
♥	KQJ10
♦	A7
♣	J3

Holding this hand you should open 1d. If your partner responds 1s you should rebid - stop 3s. If your partner responds 1h, you bid - stop 2s which will confirm your strong hand. Again if your partner responds 2c after your 1d opening, you can bid

♠	AKQJ
♥	K73
♦	J6432
♣	K

straight to game– stop 3nt knowing partner has at least 8/9 points.

♠	Q1075
♥	K7
♦	K8642
♣	AJ

You open 1d and if your partner responded 1h, you should then bid your Spades. If partner responded 1s you can support and bid 2s but should your partner bid 2c after your 1d opening, you would not be strong enough to bid the Spades at the 2 level; you would have to rebid your Diamonds. You would need 15 or more points to bid 2s. Strong opening hands holding 15 or more points are discussed later.

Exceptions to the rule – when holding two four card majors like the following hand.

♠	KQ64
♥	AQ95
♦	96
♣	KJ4

You should open 1h and not 1s. The reason is that when you open the higher of two four card major suits you may miss the opportunity of getting a fit in the lower suit and it is a shame if this happens when the lower suit is a major. Also, if you open 1s and then bid 2h you are confirming that you hold five spades which is not the case.

Another exception already mentioned is a Roman hand with 4441 shape as in the following examples: <u>Red</u> or <u>Black</u> singleton?

♠	KJ63
♥	7
♦	KQ83
♣	A642

Open 1d

Red, you open the biddable suit below but if black you open the middle of the other 3 suits. But only if suit is biddable.

♠	AQ63
♥	K843
♦	A984
♣	10

Open 1h

Exceptions now out of the way

♠	K8
♥	AKQJ
♦	8532
♣	J73

You may consider opening 1h but you should, of course, open 1nt. It's balanced and with 14 points. If you were to open 1h what then would you rebid after your partner said 1s?

On this hand you would open 1h which would confirm holding 4 Hearts and then bid the Diamonds at the 2 level which would confirm you held 5 Hearts and 4 Diamonds.

♠	A5
♥	Q9642
♦	AJ64
♣	K3

♠	KJ853
♥	J
♦	KQ952
♣	A4

Two five card Suits. You should open the higher suit first – 1s. If the two suits are black open the Club and then rebid the spades.

Your partner has opened the bidding in a suit and your RHO passes.

As the Responder – what do you do now?
Let's get the easy bit out of the way first.
If you have less than 6 points you PASS.
But occasionally you do have to be sensible.

Look at this hand

♠	Q754
♥	J7642
♦	J863
♣	void

If my partner opened 1h then holding this hand I think I would respond 2h even holding only 4 points. The void is worth a few points and my partner will find the five Hearts pretty useful as well.

You and your partner may care to come to an arrangement, agreed by many Bridge players, whereby support of a major suit opening can be given holding at least four cards and only 5 points. Some players have agreed that the five points must include an Ace or a King in the trump suit.

A message in duplicate – Just in case you forget

It is your duty to support partner's major
It is your duty to support partner's major

If your partner opens in a major 1h or 1s, you must remember that with 6 or more points, <u>it is your duty</u> to support your partner if you have 4 cards or more support even if they are miserable looking cards like the Hearts in the illustration. You may support with only 3 cards but at least two of them should be honours. Your minor suit

♠	73
♥	6532
♦	AK57
♣	964

may be better equipped with points but you must support and bid even though the 4 card support may be only 6532.

Your partner opens 1h and you hold this hand and you think your partner will not want to know about your miserable four little Hearts you will be forgetting that your partner may be sitting across the way with a strong hand and itching to bid a game in that Major. Put it this way, <u>those four pathetic cards are not held by the opposition</u>.

Partner has opened in a suit at the 1 level and your RHO passes.
<u>With 6/7 points</u> – Said yet again, if you have four cards in a major suit then show your major at the 1 level, failing which support your partner's suit at the 2 level.

Never deny a four card major

When I was learning Bridge at evening classes I responded 1nt to my partner's 1 level opening in a minor suit whilst holding four spade cards. My teacher, Ann, who was standing behind me at the time banged lightly on my head nine times with a knuckle and spoke at the same time emphasising the syllables to <u>Ne</u>-<u>ver</u> <u>de</u>-<u>ny</u> <u>a</u> <u>four</u> <u>card</u> <u>maj</u>-<u>or</u>. To my dying day I will never forget those few words.

If your partner opens in a minor suit and you have four or more cards in a major suit then bid the major at the 1 level even if you have only four miserable looking cards. Having both majors bid the

♠	5432
♥	86
♦	AKQJ
♣	952

longest suit but if equal length bid the Hearts first. Even if you have four or more card support for partner's minor bid <u>you must bid the major first</u>. **Never deny a four card major.** Holding this hand, if your partner opens 1d then <u>your response is 1s and not 2d</u>. You will have a chance to show those Diamonds after partner has rebid.

Partner has opened in a suit at the 1 level and your RHO passes.
<u>With 8/10 points</u> – still show your major at the 1 level over partner's minor or support partner at the 2 level or bid your own 5 or more card suit at the 2 level.

Partner has opened in a suit at the 1 level and your RHO passes.
<u>With 6/10 points</u> and not a suit to bid (you need at least 8 points + five cards to change suit and bid at the 2 level) then bid 1nt. You do <u>not</u> need to be balanced. But, common sense needs to prevail on occasions when you should not stick to the rules. If you have 6 or 7 points and six Hearts then bid 2h over 1s.

Many folk have an agreement that the responder must have at least 9 points to change the suit and respond at the 2 level. I respond with only 8 points as you see from the examples. There are arguments for and against. You must discuss this aspect with your partners and agree the minimum points to respond.

♠	9
♥	Q732
♦	K853
♣	Q862

You hold this miserable hand. Your partner opens 1s. What do you bid? You must bid holding at least 6 points. You lack both requirements to change the suit and call at the 2 level. <u>Less than 8 points and no five card suit</u>. You just bid 1nt and note that you do not need to be balanced when responding in no-trumps at the 1 level. However, in this instance, the opening bid has corrected the imbalance.

Another 1nt response. Your partner opens 1s and you hold this hand. You cannot support spades but you do have five Diamonds but not enough points to bid them. You only have 7 points and thus your reply to partner's 1s opening bid is – 1nt. Still not a balanced hand but to reply 1nt to a suit opening <u>you do not need to be balanced</u>.

♠	9
♥	K864
♦	A6432
♣	962

If your partner opens in a minor and you do not have a four card major but four or more card support for the minor then bid the minor at the two level – even with only 6 points. After partner's 1c or 1d bid you would bid 2c or 2d with this hand but after partner's opening bid in a major you would bid 1nt holding this hand.

♠	A72
♥	Q5
♦	9642
♣	9852

♠	5432
♥	A95
♦	Q98
♣	Q82

If your partner opens 1h and you, without 4 card Heart support hold 4 Spades then bid 1s. **Never deny a four card major** even though they may be very poor. You partner may well have 4 Spades as well but correctly bid the Hearts first.

If partner opens the bidding with 1s and you, without 4 card Spade support hold 4 hearts, with only 6/7 points you bid 1nt. After a 1s opening you should not bid 2h with only 4 cards, unless supporting partner, and particularly with less than 8 points because by doing so you would be guaranteeing 5 Hearts.

♠	974
♥	AK83
♦	986
♣	852

> If partner opens at the 1 level in Spades, you <u>must</u> have at least five Hearts cards to call that suit at the 2 level.

Still responding with 6/10 points.

♠	KJ3
♥	J642
♦	972
♣	Q97

If your partner opens in a major and you have 4 or more cards in that major suit then support at the 2 level – even with only 6/7 points. After partner's 1h bid you would bid 2h holding this hand but if partner opens 1s you will respond 1nt holding only four Heart cards.

If your partner opens 1c and you do not have 4 or more cards in a major suit but have four cards in Diamonds, then bid 1d, but only if the suit is biddable otherwise bid 1nt. unless of course, you have four clubs in which case bid 2c. In this hand the Diamonds are not worth bidding so bid 1nt.

♠	K42
♥	K64
♦	8753
♣	J53

If your partner opens 1h or 1s, you, holding this 9 point hand, cannot support and you cannot bid another suit through lack of 5 card suit, must now bid 1nt which confirms a holding of 6-10 points and if 8 or more points, not a five card suit.

♠	A76
♥	K62
♦	9874
♣	Q85

♠	AK72
♥	J865
♦	865
♣	82

If your partner opens in a minor suit and you have four or more cards in a major then bid the major at the 1 level. If you have both majors then bid the Hearts first even though the Spades are better. On this hand bid 1h.

♠	AK97
♥	9865
♦	865
♣	82

If your partner opens 1h or 1s and you have 4 or more Hearts/Spades then support and bid 2h or 2s. (the losing trick count to be discussed very soon – will amend this note).

If your partner opens 1h and you cannot support but hold 4 or more Spade cards then bid 1s. Remember, you can change the suit, with less than 8 points when bidding at the 1 level and you need only four cards.

♠	K932
♥	J54
♦	Q96
♣	942

I'll repeat - Many folk have an agreement that the responder must have at least 9 points to change the suit and respond at the 2 level. I respond with only 8 points as you see from the examples. There are arguments for and against. You must discuss this aspect with your various partners and agree the minimum points to respond.

If partner opens 1s and you cannot support but you have four hearts,

♠	Q54
♥	AQ94
♦	874
♣	J54

you should not bid hearts at the 2 level because you only hold 4 hearts. You need 5 hearts to bid 2h after partner's 1s bid, even with 8 points because a bid of 2h, after 1s will guarantee 5 Heart cards. Your partner holding 3 Heart cards will then be sure of fit. Holding this hand you should respond 1nt.

Now a diversion before a recap.
True we didn't have a train to catch and it would not have mattered if we had arrived at our daughter's house a little later than Margaret had arranged. What did matter was the time I spent in our hallway waiting for Margaret to get off the phone so that we could at least get started.

After an almost instant response to the remark *'isn't it about time you got yourself ready'* I had a shower, got dressed, combed the few locks left on my head and presented myself ready for the exodus and then presented myself for departure a second time after attaching my hearing aids. We are on the point of leaving the house and that green object in the lounge doorway rang.

I then sit in the hallway like a Charlie waiting for her ladyship to finish talking. She's talking to Pat and the subject is someone I doubted whether Pat knew but all the same Pat was hearing about it anyway and after what seemed like a lifetime, the goodbyes were being said I arose from my seat in anticipation of an imminent departure when I heard those fatal words which enquired as to the health of Pat's mum and dad. Down I sat again somewhat frustrated because I knew for a fact the conversation had not at that time reached the half way point. What was I to do?

An apple had disappeared and I was just about to go for the newspaper when the head of laundry emerged and came out with the classic remark or was it remarks in the form of first a question which was immediately followed by a command. 'Are you ready yet? You're not wearing that jumper.'

I was ready, I'd been ready for ten or so minutes but in view of the jumper I was suddenly not ready. The garment in question was not a jumper at all but that's not the point. The item of clothing was clean but the problem was that I had had the garment with the Denis the Menace motive for some years and for some reason beyond my comprehension it was now not suitable to wear on a visit to my Daughter Mandy who prefers to spell her name Mandi for some obscure reason. I changed into a sweat shirt purchased at the same time as the rejected item and everything was hunky dory.

Now that recap – open bidding at 1 level with 12/19 high card points. With 6 cards or 2x5 card suits you can open the bidding holding only 10/11 points. Remember length before strength and the Rule of 20.

If your partner has opened the bidding at the 1 level and your RHO stays silent, never pass, unless you have less than 6 points or support by partnership arrangement with only 5 points. Even holding a miserable six point hand, your partner may be sitting opposite with 19 points which with your 6 points is enough for game. Now that's a thought.

1 level suit openings and partner's replies with less than 11pts.

Opener				Responder
With enough points and that obvious suit, the opening bid is 1h.	873 KQ1098 106 AK4	♠ ♥ ♦ ♣	9654 73 AKJ9 986	Lovely diamonds but never deny a four card major and thus the response is 1s.

Opener				Responder
Another opening hand at the 1 level Diamonds are the longest so bid 1d.	AQ7 KJ5 AQ1098 J3	♠ ♥ ♦ ♣	5432 1093 KJ75 A5	Good Diamond support but with 4 cards in major, however poor, bid 1s

Opener with Roman hand 4441			Responder
With black singleton open middle of other 3 suits – open 1h	KQ98 AQ94 J1092 Q	♠ ♥ ♦ ♣	32 K106 KQ76 J952	No five card suit so just respond 1nt.

Opener			Responder
Still open at the 1 level with these 19 points – open 1h	AK7 KQ1075 KJ10 K3	♠ ♥ ♦ ♣	108 J863 A2 J9865	In contrast, what a pathetic hand. Only 6 points but support so bid 2h.

Opener			Responder
14 points and length in Spades – bid 1s	Q9842 QJ105 K8 AQ	♠ ♥ ♦ ♣	A1053 986 J743 32	Pass, unless you have agreed to respond with only 5 points in which case bid 2s.

Opener			Responder
4x4 in majors, open Hearts first. If you open Spades first and then bid Hearts you show 5 Spades	AQJ10 9632 K75 AJ	♠ ♥ ♦ ♣	763 KJ8 AQ9 8765	10 points but no five card suit so just bid 1nt.

Opener			Responder
Only 10 points but with 6 Heart cards open 1h	865 AJ8763 K7 Q5	♠ ♥ ♦ ♣	J942 KQ 9654 763	Good honours in partner's suit but with 4 spades respond 1s.

Open the higher sequence of two five card suits. Open 1h in spite of the Clubs being much stronger.	K8 98652 6 AKQ74	♠ ♥ ♦ ♣	KJ75 AJ74 985 52	Support partner major with four cards. Respond 2h. Do not bid 1s.

11 points and Rule of 20 passed. Those two suits are just too ropey. Best pass holding this hand.	J QJ74 QJ852 A74	♠ ♥ ♦ ♣	AQ742 652 A7 K83	If RHO passes open 1s or overcall 1s after 1 level opening by RHO.

Many less experienced players will not bid unless they have at least 12 points and that policy cost two opposition pairs dearly at my local club for not opening the bidding holding 6 cards in a minor and 10 points. Whilst the opposition were able to bid 4s in any event, the player on lead was the partner of the player who should have opened 1d. Not having knowledge of the Diamond cards opposite, another suit, which well suited the opposition, was led and the contract made easily with overtricks. With knowledge, the lead would have been a Diamond and the Defenders would have taken the first three tricks, the third trick with an over-ruff. <u>If you do not tell your partner, how is your partner to know?</u>

> When sitting there looking at your pathetic hand, just remember that you do have a partner sitting opposite. Don't think
> *'I cannot do anything'*
> but think
> **'can we do anything'**
> and remember your bid may give your partner a valuable lead indicator.

In the early editions of my last book *The Road Across the Bridge*, page 49 to be exact, I showed the following illustrated hand and this bidding suggestion which I later realised might have been wrong or was it?

♠	Void
♥	KQ1098
♦	KQ3
♣	K7643

You hold this hand and partner has opened 1nt. The void in spades makes the hand most unsuitable for a no trump contract. Try Stayman hoping for a heart reply, in which case bid to game - 4h. If reply is the negative 2d bid 3h but if reply is 2s then bid 3nt.

After publication of the first book I considered a better solution should be as follows:

> You should simply bid stop 3h which is forcing to game and leaves the final decision to your partner who will either bid 3nt or 4h.

In searching for an excuse for my first bidding suggestion I must admit that even if partner had a poor 1nt opener, like this hand, the response should have perhaps been stop 3h and it would be most unfortunate if partner then bid 3nt holding this hand

♠	Q95
♥	J7
♦	A942
♣	AJ53

on the basis that Qxx was a stop. The Declarer will be slaughtered in a 3nt contract.

In search of comfort I set the responder hand out on a sheet of paper and asked ten very experienced players at my local clubs. Half the players I approached suggested the Stayman route was best and the other half said they would respond -stop 3h. I am now relaxed that my first suggestion will not be criticised too much but to be honest with you, having now considered further, I think I would now respond stop 3h and leave partner to decide.

I wrote to one of the Bridge magazines and the official answer to the question was that the responder should bid - stop 3h.

Enjoying drinks with friends the other evening, a lady mentioned that she had been criticised for not opening with 12 points which comprised three Aces and she asked what I thought. My reply was very simple. 'Suppose you passed and your partner also had a miserable looking 12 point hand and passed as well.' If my partner has just three Aces then I would always want to know.

I play bridge at two local clubs two or three times a week. One club on Monday and Friday evenings and at another club on .... excuse me for a moment.

I'm trying to give you an account of my Bridge movements each week and I've suddenly got Margaret at my side with a pair of scissors having noticed a long hair on my left eyebrow and it's got me thinking about our television handset. Don't ask me why. The handset we have is quite fantastic. It seems to control not only the television but also Margaret's volume because when I touch the button to increase the level of sound given out by the TV set the volume on Margaret's voice also increases. The more I raise the volume on the TV the louder Margaret's voice gets – it's quite amazing. There is however one big disappointment. The off button affects only the TV set.

I wish Margaret would buy bread that fits the toaster.

CHAPTER

Opener's Rebid
holding less than 15points
+ Losing Trick Count
+ Distribution Points

Your opening hand at the 1 level will hold between 10 and 19 points and if only 10 or 11 points the hand will hold either a six card suit or two five card suits making up two distribution points or you have opened using the Rule of 20 with two suits split 5/4 by adding the number of cards to the HCP's in hand to equal 20.

Now divide that opening hand into three sections.
10-14 points – a weak opening hand
15-17 points – a strong opening hand
18-19 points - a very strong opening hand

Three things you must <u>not do</u> when holding a weak opening hand.

Firstly - You must <u>not rebid</u> above two of your opened suit called a <u>Suit Reverse</u>, unless supporting your partner. I call the suit reverse, *Jumping over your Fence*. Open 1 of a suit and your fence is 2 of that suit and a rebid the other side of your fence means that you have a strong or very strong hand. Do not bid a second suit which is, in sequence, above that of your first bid suit. For example do not open 1d and then bid 2h after your partner responds 2c because you would have bid beyond your 2d fence holding a weak opening hand.

Secondly - Do not jump in your opening bid suit. If you open 1h and your partner bids 1s do not then bid 3h even though you may have 6 hearts. You must have a strong or very strong opening hand to jump.

Thirdly – Do not reverse into no-trumps. To open in a suit and then rebid in no-trumps shows more than 14 points.

Remember that when supporting your opening bid suit at the 2 level, your partner is only guaranteeing 6 points (or 5 points by arrangement) so be careful and consider **one up – shut up**.

The Losing Trick Count

If you are able to support (at least four cards) your partner's opening 1 level major suit bid then count your losers and add that figure to partner's assumed 7 losers. Take the total from 18 and consider a bid of the major suit at that level. You will often find that even with less than 11 points you can jump bid.

Or

Forget your partner's assumed losers and deduct your losers from 11

How to Count Losers

A void or singleton ace – no losers.

Any other singleton count 1 loser
or an Ace or King doubleton (Ax) (Kx) count 1 loser.

Any other doubleton count 2 losers.

With AJ10 just count 1 loser
But with Qxx count as 2 losers only if partner has bid the suit
otherwise count as 3 losers.

Any three card or longer suit without the AKQ count as 3 losers.

Do not count more than 3 losers in any suit.

With 5 card support then deduct 1 loser.

Counting the losers in the following hands.
On each hand your partner has opened 1h.

♠	974	3 losers
♥	AK83	1 loser
♦	986	3 losers
♣	852	3 losers

This is a ten losing trick hand and thus considered quite weak. You would just support and bid 2h.

♠	Q	1 loser
♥	AK832	0 losers
♦	QJ862	2 losers
♣	85	2 losers

This 5 losing trick hand is significantly stronger. As there are five Heart cards, one loser is removed hence there are no Heart losers. Holding this hand after partner's 1h opening you could bid to game – stop 4h but a bid of stop 3h would be prudent, showing your strength and leaving partner to make the final decision.

♠	AJ10	1 loser
♥	9832	3 losers
♦	Q98	3 losers
♣	K73	2 losers

Only 1 loser in Spades because of the Jack ten sequence. With AJ9 there would be 2 losers. With Heart support and nine losers, after partner's 1h opening, holding this hand you would bid 2h.

Additional Points for Distribution

Once you have established a trump suit you can add points for distribution. With a void add 3 with a singleton add 2 and with a doubleton add 1 point but only add points on those suits which have not been bid by partner. Only add these points when you are about to support your partner's suit. Very useful when considering whether or not to raise to game.

Your Rebid Showing Five Cards in your Opening Suit.

Don't rebid your opening suit just to show five cards when you have another biddable suit of four cards in sequence below that of your first suit.

Remember when you rebid your opening suit you confirm at least five cards in that suit. Promising only four cards in the opening bid, a rebid of that suit confirms at least one more card. If you have a second biddable suit in sequence below that of your first suit and less than 15 points, a bid of that suit at the 2 level will usually show a holding of at least five cards in the suit you opened. This is very economical bidding because you have not only shown length in your first suit but also a second suit in one bid.

Some examples of the opener's rebid after a response from partner.

Opener				Responder
Opening 1d	KQ73	♠	85	1h
	A	♥	K643	
Rebid – 1s	K8542	♦	Q73	
	J95	♣	Q842	1nt.

After the 1d opening the response of 1h shows neither weakness nor strength but at least 6 points and of course, at least four Hearts. With only 13 points the opener holds a weak hand and as such the rebid will not be higher than 2 of opening suit. As the responder has bid 1h then the opener can now show those four Spades at the 1 level and bid 1s. The responder is not interested in either Diamonds or Spades and partner has not shown any interest in Hearts so the responder will finish off in 1nt having cover in the unbid suit. Although partner has confirmed 5 Diamond cards and 3 Diamonds are held in hand, a 1nt contract, if made, is much better than 2d especially if extra tricks are made.

Opener					Responder
Opening 1d	KQ73	♠	8542		1h
	A	♥	K643		
Rebid – 1s	K8542	♦	Q73		Rebid 2s
	J95	♣	Q8		
Pass					

Length before strength, opener bids 1d and responder with four cards in both majors bids the Hearts not denying holding 4 spades. The opener, holding a weak opening hand, will rebid 1s and the responder will bid 2s confirming a fit and knowing that partner has a weak opening hand which is now reconfirmed by the opener's pass.

Opener					Responder
Opens 1h	K8	♠	A952		Stop 3h
	A7543	♥	K986		
Rebid – 4h.	5	♦	J986		
	K7542	♣	3		pass

Opener has only 10 points but 2 x 5 card suits so the opening bid is 1h. The responder has four card Heart support and with eight losers after calculating the losing tricks, bids an encouraging 3h. The opener, although weak in terms of HCP's has that singleton and a doubleton which now makes the hand somewhat stronger and the opener finishes off in 4h.

Opener					Responder
Opens 1d	K9	♠	7843		1s
	98	♥	Q43		
Rebid – 2d	KQ7642	♦	J9853		Pass.
	Q82	♣	K		

With 10 points and six cards opener bids 1d. The responder has good Diamond support but having also four cards in a major, however miserable they are, will never deny a four card major and will therefore bid 1s. The opener will rebid the Diamonds at the 2 level which confirms a weak opening hand and at least five Diamonds. Responder passes with those 6 points, not giving partner any encouragement because game in Diamonds is a long way off.

Opener				Responder
Opens 1d	Q982	♠	J54	Reply 1nt.
	A	♥	J43	
pass	KQ762	♦	J4	
	982	♣	A10754	

With 11 points and two suits 5/4 the opening bid is 1d under the Rule of 20. 11 HCP's plus the cards in the two long suits = 20. The responder with only 7 points should not bid 2c but replies 1nt and with that the opener passes knowing full well that partner does not have four Spades to support those in hand.

How does opener know partner most definitely does not have four Spades? Because partner would <u>never deny a four card major</u>.

N	Opener	S	Responder
♠	KQ763	♠	J1092
♥	K	♥	A10982
♦	764	♦	KQ82
♣	AJ32	♣	void

North has 13 points and not being suitable for opening 1nt will open 1s. South has 5 Hearts but can support Spades and with only 6 losers will bid straight to game – stop 4s. That void in clubs is so valuable.

South's losers?
Spades = 3   (AKQ)
Hearts = 2   (KQ)
Diamonds = 1   (A)
Clubs – None   (void)
6 losers + partner's assumed 7 = 13 from 18 = 5
No point in bidding 5 so just settle for game and bid 4s.

Run through these four responder hands and count the losers and consider the bid after your partner has opened 1h.

♠	KJ3	2 losers
♥	J642	3 losers
♦	Q72	3 losers (if partner has not bid this suit).
♣	974	3 losers

11 losers so just bid 2h.

♠	Void	No losers
♥	K753	2 losers
♦	AK642	1 loser
♣	9753	3 losers

6 losers so bid straight to game – 4h

♠	A93	2 losers
♥	AQ42	1 loser
♦	972	3 losers
♣	862	3 losers

9 losers so just bid 2h.

♠	A83	2 losers
♥	AQ753	1 loser – less 1 loser for the fifth card.
♦	97	2 losers
♣	862	3 losers making a total of 7 losers.

With only 7 losers you may like to bid stop 4h but if vulnerable and perhaps a little cautious because of those ropey cards in the minors, then I suggest you bid stop 3h. If not vulnerable you could be a little bullish and bid 4h and then find your partner has three losing Clubs and a losing Diamond. Just can't win sometimes.

Maybe a very negative thought - But
Before making a decision as to game after counting your losers always consider the vulnerability and also the fact that your partner's trump cards may not be of particularly good quality and the hand may only have 12 points. Perhaps I'm being too negative.

I've been clearing out a cupboard in my den and found an old Council Tax bill which is now in the wpb or should I say on the floor next to the wpb. The address at the top of the bill caught my eye.

Mid Sussex District Council
PO Box 119
Council Offices
Oaklands,
Oaklands Road
Haywards Heath
West Sussex
RH16 1SW

Can you believe it? Eight lines. Of course you can. Just in case the post office was in any doubt about the location of the council offices I suggest another few lines   like -- South and just up from the railway station just past and on the other side of the road from the Job Centre.

When I receive that mass of paper that passes through my letter box most mornings I divide the items into two piles and very occasionally three piles. The third pile which occurs following a blue moon is the £50 win from ERNIE. The first pile destined for almost immediate deposit in the recycling bin comprise all the coloured advertising items, all items marked 'urgent' and 'open immediately'. Also in that pile are those envelopes without an address and those where the address label is about 45 degrees off the horizontal which makes me assume in any event that the sender had little interest in my opening the envelope.

By the way, wpb mentioned means waste paper bin. Why I should have assumed you would know what I was talking about I do not know. My Brother John used to be a policeman and his speech often contained many RTA's and GBH's and sometimes I would reply with WTDAYTA, which in simple Stephens language is 'what the dickens are you talking about'. It's fine when folk of the same profession are talking to one another but I don't want those suffering from abreviationicaria or acronymitis talking to me.

There are many recognised acronyms in Bridge and one caught my eye the other day – PLOB meaning Petty, Little, Odious Bid which is an investigative rebid by responder after 1nt rebid by partner.   I'm off - TTFN.

CHAPTER 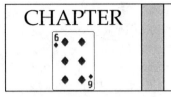	The Simple Suit Overcall The No-Trump Overcall The Jump Overcall

The Simple Suit Overcall

I consider a 1 level overcall in a suit holding a minimum of 8 points but many partnerships insist on having 9 or 10 points, the latter I feel being somewhat restrictive. You and your partner must decide. The notes that follow are based on a suit overcall at the 1 level holding a minimum of 8 points. It is important that you discuss the minimum points of an overcall with your partner before you start playing.

> Whilst suggesting that you may overcall with only 8 points, I emphasise that if you only have 8 or 9 points, you should ensure that you pass the **suit overcall test** mentioned below before you bid, especially if you are vulnerable.

To overcall in a suit
you need at least **five** cards in the overcall suit.

To overcall at the 1 level = 8/15 pts

To overcall at the 2 level = 10/15 pts

and

To overcall at the 3 level then 12/15pts.

If you are at the lower end of the overcall points scale, do what I call The Suit Overcall Test. If you are in some doubt as to whether to overcall because your hand looks a little weak, add the number of cards in your planned overcall suit to the number of honours in that suit and if the total equals or exceeds the number of tricks already bid, then overcall otherwise it may be wise to stay quiet. If your only honour in the suit is a Jack then do not count that honour.

To overcall 1 no-trump you do need 15/18 points and obviously a good stop or two in any suit bid by the opposition would be very prudent to say the least and best you do not consider Qxx a reasonable stop.

What if your partner has overcalled - the facts are as follows:
If the overcall is at the 1 level then in the hand opposite you there are at least 5 cards in the suit and 8-15 points. A 2 level overcall means that there are at least 5 cards and 10-15 points and a 3 level overcall means a minimum of five cards and at least 12 points. The need to respond to your partner's overcall is not as great as when your partner has opened the bidding and if you have at least 3 cards in partner's overcall suit then you have a fit unlike the responder of an opening hand who needs 4 cards to support.

If you are very weak say with only 4/5 points you will have nothing to say then say nothing – pass. With 6/7 points only bid to support your partner and you will need at least three cards to support. If you have a few more points and no support for partner but at least a couple of stops in the opening suit then perhaps consider bidding no-trumps. Don't forget when considering whether or not you have stops in the left hand opponent's suit that the lead of that suit may to come from your right hand side which could create a problem. Holding KJxx should not be considered a stop because of the likelihood of the LHO having AQxx and anything you play will be squashed.

Unless you are quite strong in another suit, best not bid your own suit if you have support for your partner's overcall suit. Remember your partner does have at least five cards in the suit so be careful about going off on your own into the wilderness because your partner may not have any cards of any significance in your suit and perish the thought; your partner may even be void in your suit.

Supporting your partner in spades will push the opponents to the next level if they want to continue bidding.

When the overcall suit is Spades then seriously consider supporting partner when holding three Spades, even with a few points because your bid will force the opposition to the next level which may be uncomfortable for them. Consider the opposition opening bid of 1h and your partner overcalling 1s. If you bid 2s holding at least three card Spade support, the opposition now have to think about bidding at the 3 level to stay in the auction.

BUT consider the down side

You may cause your partner to continue in the auction believing you have good support. Therefore be careful when forcing the opposition to bid especially when your side is vulnerable.

If you've 11 or more points and a couple of good stops in opener's suit, taking into account what I said on the subject of stops and you are sitting in the fourth position after your partner has overcalled, you might like to consider bidding the opener's suit at the next level.

What!! Bidding opposition opening suit.

It is a conventional bid because you are not bidding the suit because you want the contract to be in that suit but you are asking your partner, with a no trump bid in mind, to confirm strength of the overcall hand. Your partner should alert the bid and bid own suit again at the next level with points at the lower end of the overcall point range, 8-11 which partner will pass or bid another suit with points at the higher end of the overcall point range, 12-15. That will encourage partner to bid game in no trumps or partner's overcall suit.

If your partner has overcalled in a minor suit and you have a few points yourself, plus stops in unmentioned suits and cover in the opponent's suit or suits, you should consider no-trumps rather than game in the minor when 11 tricks are required to win the contract.

After a couple of years at two adult education Bridge courses and umpteen lessons on the same subject at home with you know who, I am sometimes confronted with a question from Margaret when playing socially, as to whether the overcall she had just made was correct. My first reaction is 'how the dickens do I know, I'm not a mind reader.' I just have to ask Margaret three questions:

1. Do you have five cards in your suit?
2. Do you have 8-15 points for 1 level overcall or 10-15 points for a two level overcall?
3. If at the lower end of point scale – have you passed the suit overcall test?

Usually what happens then is that Margaret removes her bid and replaces it with a pass so then the opposition have pretty good ideas about Margaret's hand.

The 1nt Overcall – By implication the 1nt overcall follows a suit bid by the opposition and the caller will have not only a stop or two in the opening bid suit but also a strong hand which means 15/18 points. Obviously in an ideal world the hand will have good cards in all the other suits as well.

If your partner has overcalled 1nt then your job is easy. Your partner has the opener's suit adequately covered, that's for sure + 15/18 points so you just bid according to your hand. With no length in any suit and less than 7 points then pass but if you have 7/8 points then bid an invitational 2nt but if you have 9 or more points then bid 3nt. If you have more than 7 points and respectable length in a major then bid that major but if the long suit is a minor then consider staying in no-trumps. Some partnerships will use Stayman after a 1nt overcall.

The Jump Overcall -If you have a strong hand with 15 or more points and six cards you can <u>jump overcall</u> which conveys two significant things to your partner.

a). 15+ points (some partnerships demand 16 points)

and

b). Six cards in the suit bid.

After the opposition have bid say 1s you would jump in your suit and bid stop 3h or after 1d you would overcall stop 2h. Your partner now knows you have six Hearts and 15+ points and therefore needs only two Heart cards for a partnership fit in Hearts. If the opposition open 1s then a jump overcall would be any bid at the three level.

8 Versus 9

Throughout my book I have advocated overcalling at the 1 level holding only 8 points. Many folk do not overcall unless they have at least 9 points and I have heard several very experienced players doubting the wisdom of overcalling with less than 9 points.

In my defence I have always made it clear that if you are at the lower end of your overcall point range then do what I call the Suit Overcall Test by adding the number of cards you have in the overcall suit to the number of honours in that suit and the answer will be the number of tricks. If that number equals or exceeds tricks already bid then overcall. <u>If the overcall test fails then pass</u>. Many times I have had more than 8 points and the suit overcall test has failed so I have passed. Do whatever your partnership agrees.

In my defence your honour…………………..

A Lead Directing Overcall Bid Holding only 6 Points!!!

In The Times, 26th October 2007, the correspondent showed a set of hands where North opened 1d and East overcalled 1h holding five Hearts including the KQ10 and a total of only 6 points in hand and South with good cover in Hearts and the other suits covered and 13 points bid 3nt and that was the contract. The correspondent mentioned that there were those who would baulk at that light overcall but the message was that such lead-directing bids are winning bridge.

Provided you pass the Suit Overcall Test I see no reason why you should not overcall with only 8 points. It will show your partner that you have a suit with some quality and perhaps provide a useful lead indicator.

I rest my case your honour.

On the subject of Honours

My blind friend has been award the O.B.E in the Queen's Birthday Honours. I am delighted for him and he well deserved the award for his services to the blind. I quite like the way he uses his finger as a measure when pouring out a malt into a long glass. That aside, my friend enthusiastically shared my view that so many people in this land who deserved an award for their unpaid services were not recognised. How unfair.

Joseph Bloggs got himself an award for special services done in work time. He worked for the Civil Service for 20 years and kept his nose clean. Well done Joe – you deserved that award. Did he heck. Presumably he received a monthly pay cheque, took regular holidays of greater length than other sector employees, took time off when sick and as he progressed through his career he took all the perks that came his way. I expect Joe was awarded for services that were expected of him when he first took on the employment.

My Father worked in the private sector for one employer for all his long working life. He was rarely late for work and took time off only when genuinely unwell. He retired at 65 having given his employers 100% support throughout. Yes he was awarded, not in any New Year Honours list or Queen's Birthday Honours but by me.

He died without an honour. On leaving the Orphan Working School & Alexandra Orphanage at Maitland Park, Haverstock Hill, London N.W in 1922, he joined a company in the West end of London and worked there for almost 50 years. He was very well respected by everyone and always considered others before himself. He had a BBC newsreaders voice and he would often pick up the telephone and be told that the call was just to hear him speak. He would never go to the loo or the toilet, it was always the lavatory.

'Sir' Reginald William Stephens – I applaud you.

I do agree with honours but at the same time I do agree with fair play and both must go together. As it would be impossible for fair play to be exercised because of sheer volumes then the New Year Honours and the Queen's Birthday Honours should be abolished.

Why should a person who has given 20 years to an establishment, been well paid and spent that time within a warm office be awarded whilst a chap who has trudged miles every day in all weathers and been a local hero in his community is totally ignored.

Off the soap box now and back to the task in hand.

> It was once said that there are three kinds of Bridge Player – Those who can count and those who can't.

A 1nt overcall confirms a window of points and partner is able to bid to 3nt with some confidence. East only had two points but the lead spells trouble for the opponents.

```
              N      ♠  KJ7
                     ♥  KJ7
                     ♦  KQ106
      W              ♣  QJ10
 ♠  A32                              ♠  Q1096
 ♥  A10865     Dealer                ♥  932
 ♦  J          West                  ♦  9872
 ♣  A876                             ♣  54
                     ♠  854                     E
                     ♥  Q4
                     ♦  A543
                     ♣  K932    S
```

The Bidding

West opens 1h.

North overcalls 1nt.

East passes.

South bids 3nt.

All then pass.

A straight forward opening bid by West.

North has a strong hand and also cover in the opposition Heart bid and a good distribution of the other suits. North bids 1nt and a bemused East passes.

South has been given some very useful information by partner. The 1nt overcall bid by North will always mean a strong hand holding 15-18 points and most important, a good stop in the opposition bid suit. South, having 9 points in hand, will immediately bid to game – stop 3nt. You may wonder why South is not concerned about the Spades holding only the 854. South considered the poor Spade holding but took the view that the opposition have not bid Spades and partner opposite has 15-18 points so there is a good chance the Spades are covered.

East is on lead. Partner has bid Hearts so East will start the process of removing Hearts from the opposition hands. East leads the 9♥ being the highest Heart because East does not want to be in a situation where the 9♥ takes a trick in the third round of Hearts and then having none to lead to partner's possible winners. Another reason for leading the 9♥ is to help draw out higher opposition cards. Every little helps so the expression goes. If West takes the trick with the Ace and then leads another Heart, the process of drawing opposition Hearts will be well under way and West still has two Aces in hand for entries to the two winning Hearts that will remain in hand. Looks to me like a one trick defeat.

CHAPTER

Some Take-Out Doubles
+
The Penalty Double after 1nt

The double of a suit for penalties will be discussed later

Negative Doubles, Informatory Doubles or Take-Out Doubles, call them what you like are very common in modern bidding. There are several variations but I practice just five which I will explain. After a suit bid by the opposition, the Take-Out Double as opposed to the Penalty Double (covered later in this book) is not a telling bid but an asking bid and requires partner to take some action unless Doubler's LHO bids in which case the Doubler's partner responds discretionally.

All Doubles of suit bids up to and including 2s are for take out. A double of any no-trump bid is for penalties as is the double of any suit bid after a no-trump bid has been doubled.

It is said that the Negative Double, as it was originally called, when invented in 1957 by Alvin Roth in his partnership with Tobias Stone, was referred to as a Sputnik Double because in that year the Soviet Union launched their Satellite called Sputnik. The Satellite was considered innovative as was the introduction of the Negative Double later that year hence the reference to Sputnik.

It appears that through common usage of the various forms of the Take–Out Double, the Sputnik Double now seems to relate only to where a suit bid cannot be made because the RHO has stolen the bidding space and best used when the responder wants to bid 1h. For example. Your partner opens 1c and you want to bid 1h but cannot because your RHO has come in with a bid of 1s. You are too weak to bid 2h so the remedy is to Double which says to partner:

- • I wanted to bid 1h
- • I am too weak to bid 2h.

The Take-Out Double 1 - Your partner opens 1h and your RHO bids 1s and you Double holding the other two suits in this case the minors. When partner opens 1c and your RHO bids 1d then your Double will show both major suits. Sitting in the fourth position after two suits have been bid by the opposition and partner has passed then the Double will mean that the other two suits are held.

The Take-Out Double 2 - Your LHO opened 1d, your partner passes and your RHO responds 1h. Holding this hand you would Double which merely tells your partner that you have an opening hand or near and have quality cards in the unbid suits ideally 5/5 or at worst 5/4. Your partner will then bid the best of the unbid suits in hand unless of course the opener rebids when your partner will bid discretionally.

♠	KJ943
♥	7
♦	J8
♣	AQ874

The Take-Out Double 3 - This is the simplest Double. After my partner bids say 1d and my RHO bids 1h I would Double holding four Spade cards but as little as 6 points. Put it this way; if my RHO had not bid 1h I would have responded 1s to my partner holding this hand. The double indicates at least four Spades and a weak hand. A bid of 1s after the 1h overcall would show 5 spades.

♠	KJ75
♥	97
♦	732
♣	Q862

The Take-Out Double 4. Often referred to as the Sputnik Double -
Your RHO has overcalled after your partner's opening bid and the overcall has stolen your bidding space. This usually happens after a minor opening by your partner and a 1s bid by your RHO as in the example. Your partner opens 1d; you wanted to bid 1h but cannot because your RHO has overcalled 1s. Not strong enough to bid Hearts at the two level, you Double which tells partner that you would have bid 1h had it not been for the interference on your right hand side. Provided there is not a 2s bid by West then North will bid 2h knowing there is a weak hand opposite but a fit in Hearts.

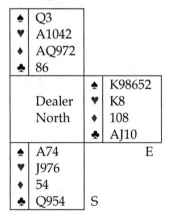

The Take-Out Double 5 – by far the most common.

It is a Double after one of the opposition have bid a suit and your partner has either not bid or has passed. You have an opening or near opening hand yourself but <u>a shortage in the suit bid by the opposition</u>. By a shortage I mean, a void, or a singleton or no more than two cards in the opposition bid suit. In an ideal world you will have quality cards in the unbid suits and as the Double asks your partner to bid best suit, you should not be too worried about what suit your partner bids. The best distribution is a 4441 hand where the singleton is the opposition opening suit. Look at this hand. Suppose the opposition have opened 1c. You are unable to overcall in a suit through lack of the required 5 cards but you are interested in what cards are opposite in your partner's hand so you Double and

♠	QJ62
♥	KJ86
♦	AJ9
♣	62

unless your LHO bids, your partner will most definitely reply even holding a Yarborough.

If you double after a minor bid by the opposition you will be holding at least 4 cards in both majors and if a major is bid by the opposition you will be holding at least four cards in the other major.

♠	753
♥	A872
♦	Q64
♣	J87

Your partner has Doubled an opening bid of say 1c and you hold this hand. You do what your partner has asked and bid your best suit which is Hearts but not necessarily at the next level. Before you reply 1h, consider the number of losers in your hand. Your partner will have an opening or near opening hand with about 7 losers and if you have an 8 loser hand, then jump 1 level and if you have 7 losers then double jump but do not bid higher than the 3 level. However it is most likely you will have 9 or more losers, as in the hand illustrated, so the reply to your partner's Double after a 1c opening in this instance will be 1h. If your partner had Doubled after an opposition 1s opening then your reply to your partner would be 2h. However if your RHO has bid then your reply to your partner's Double is discretional.

♠	AQ752
♥	97
♦	96
♣	9874

Your partner has Doubled a 1d opening bid and you now hold this hand. Your partner has asked you to bid your best suit and obviously your Spades are going to be shown but at what level. You have 8 losers in your hand so you jump one level and reply stop 2s.

♠	975
♥	KQ53
♦	942
♣	J63

The opposition have opened 1h and your partner has Doubled. Holding this hand you just bid 1nt which will confirm that you hold cards in the opponent's suit. Your partner may then leave you in that contract having cover in the other suits.

♠	A
♥	KQ953
♦	975
♣	J863

Your LHO opened 1s. Your partner has Doubled and your RHO has passed.   This is a 7 loser hand. No losing spades, 1 losing Heart, 3 losing Diamonds and 3 losing Clubs. You will tell your partner about this interesting hand by bidding stop 3h knowing that your partner must have at least four Hearts having Doubled after a 1s bid.

♠	J75
♥	7532
♦	942
♣	963

Your partner has Doubled and your RHO has passed. You must bid even holding this miserable hand because if not, the Take-Out Double will convert to a Penalty Double if your LHO passes as well. If your LHO opened 1c or 1d then your reluctant answer to your partner's Double is 1h. Suppose your LHO had opened 1s and your partner Doubled – what then? Unless your RHO has bid something after partner's Double then you must say something and even holding this horrible hand you must do what your partner has asked and you bid your best suit - 2h.

What do you do when your partner has Doubled and the opener's partner has bid? The bid by the opener's partner has removed the Double aspect from the auction so, strictly speaking, you do not have to do anything. If you have nothing to say like holding the hand immediately above then say nothing and pass but if you are West on the next illustration then you would certainly want to say something to your partner even holding the weak hand shown.

North will open 1d.
East will Double.
South will respond 2d.
Now what does West do?

	N	♠	Q10		
		♥	A1042		
		♦	AQ972		
W		♣	86		
♠	J9654			♠	A873
♥	653	Dealer		♥	KJ7
♦	K3	North		♦	65
♣	J107			♣	AK94
		♠	K2		E
		♥	Q98		
		♦	J1084		
		♣	Q532	S	

As South has bid then there is now no need for West to bid because the Double has been removed and there is now no risk that the take-out aspect of the Double will convert to a Penalty Double. However those five Spades in that miserable looking hand are significant and West recalls that whilst partner is short of Diamonds, cards will be held in the other three suits particularly the majors after a minor opening. West must bid 2s especially if West has got to rely on partner for a lift home.

After partner's support and West's 2s bid, North will bid 3d and East will bid 3s and that will be that. West will not bid to game because a better hand than the one already indicated cannot be shown.

If your partner has Doubled, asking you to bid your best suit and your RHO makes a bid, then reply to your partner's request at your discretion. Don't forget, your partner is looking for support and wants you to say something so only pass when you think that is a prudent move. If the opposition have bid a minor and you have a four card major, a suit not bid by your RHO, your partner will want to know.

> If after the Double, the opener or opener's partner win the contract, the position of opening or near opening points will be known which will make for some good finessing opportunities.

With all the above in mind, if my partner Doubles, I add my losers and often the result will be 9 or more. After all the opener has bid with opening points and my partner has Doubled, again with opening points or near so there cannot be too many points left. However if after adding my losers, I have 8 losers, I consider a jump bid and if I have seven losers I will generally bid at the three level but never more unless I have an opening hand myself.

If your partner has doubled, the message to you is simple but be sensible and just consider the situation for a moment even holding no points at all – a Yarborough.

If the opposition have opened 1h and your partner has Doubled

♠	987543
♥	void
♦	97652
♣	98

and your RHO bids stop 3h then what do you imagine you should bid holding this hand? A player holding this hand the other evening and without any thought for his partner passed. If only the player holding this hand had thought for a moment and questioned – *'would my partner who has Doubled be at all interested in my Yarborough and six miserable Spades?'* The score sheet or the traveller as it is called showed a 4s contract being made. The ruffing prospects in the hand are so significant as are the long Spades. Holding this hand after partner has doubled a 1 level opening suit bid of anything bar Spades then you must show those Spades. Your partner will most definitely want to know about them.

"The hall needs painting" were words uttered by Mrs M. Stephens, as she retreated after depositing a very welcome mug of coffee. Five minutes earlier, whilst I was trying to explain the Take-Out Double when sitting in the fourth position holding two unbid suits, we had a short discussion as to whether we should insure ourselves should any of our teeth be removed because of an accident. When I say discussion I actually mean fifty, sixty or perhaps it was two hundred words from Margaret and one word from me and that word being - No. I uttered twice as many words when responding to the comment about the hall needing painting – "I know." I can now get back to Doubling with the knowledge that I will not covered for insurance if I get my teeth knocked out and that the question about the hall being painted has reared its ugly head again.

I've noticed a bottle of beer on my shelf which my son John bought me. The yellow label says – Fertility Ale and the ABV printed on the bottle is 4.7%, whatever ABV stands for. I have a book called Abbreviations, Signs and Symbols in Common Use. Obviously ABV is not a common abbreviation but I can see A.B.S – able bodied seaman and Abp for archbishop but nothing for ABV. However what does it matter. As long as the strength is 4.7% then who cares what the ABV stands for because after a few bottles, I imagine Advanced Bloody Vandal would be apt.

There is a preponderance of over 65's playing Bridge today and looking at some of the faces at the various clubs I visit I would suggest the figure is nearer the 80's and when they play difficult hands the word that comes to mind is - centenarians. The falling off rate compared with the stepping on rate is quite high, I would imagine and if newcomers are not introduced at a higher rate than is apparent today then the demise of Bridge could well be on the cards.

We need more youngsters. The other week, as a bit of a joke, I asked my eight year old grand-daughter Lucia whether she would like to learn to play Bridge. She is a very bright young lady who sucks up knowledge like a sponge. Lucia and I have many hours of card play under our belts playing games like *Beat your Neighbour*, *Rummy*, and *Pontoon* with match-sticks taking the place of coins. Her mother Mandy, not aware of the games of Pontoon I hasten to add, had previously announced that she wanted Lucia to 'have a life' and as such, lessons in Bridge would not be a good idea. Anyway I had a quiet word with Lucia who agreed to have some tuition and to date I have spent three short sessions with her on Bridge ground works. The points for the honour cards, the number of points in a suit and in a pack of cards and identifying the Declarer in early minibridge exercises. Early days for sure but I do hope she will be able to partner me before my days are out.

I have reproduced a letter I received from Lucia.

To Grandad

Thank you for my bridge lessons and I am looking forward to my next one. I realy enjoyed our ride in the sports car. In bridge

I Learned that in a suit there are 10 points and in a pack there are 40 points.

Love from
Lucia
XXX

You'll have noticed the reference to the sports car. *"Why do you need a sports car when you've already got a car? – it'll be a five minute wonder and what a waste of money"*. That was two years ago from a lady still trying to get to grips with Bridge and who would never consider driving a car that did not have automatic gears. Margaret comes out in the MX5 occasionally and always feels the need to hold on for dear life when I corner at 30mph.

The Re-Double - Your partner's opening suit bid at the 1 level has been Doubled. The Double is normally for take-out but you should check if in any doubt. At your turn to bid ask the Doubler's partner what the bid meant. If the Double is for take-out then it will be of little concern and you should respond to your partner as normal. At least you know where an opening or near opening opposition hand is located and perhaps you can do some point counting.

If you cannot support your partner's suit or bid something yourself and have about 10 points you can Re-Double which merely tells your partner just that you have about 10 points yourself which should give your partner some confidence of making a further bid in the light of the Double on partner's left hand side.

The Doubler's partner will pass at his/her peril because if the Re-Double remains, penalty points will apply and it certainly was not the intention of the Doubler for the Double to remain let alone a Re-Double. The Doubler has asked partner to bid best suit. Unless the Double is taken off by an opposition bid then the Doubler's partner must bid something other than a pass, even holding a Yarborough.

The Penalty Double after 1nt - The opposition have opened 1nt and you have 15-18 points so you Double (a Penalty Double) hoping that your partner has at least six HCP's failing which your partner will rescue and bid a suit to remove the Double. You Doubled on the basis the 1nt opening bid was the weak kind with 12-14 points and not a strong no-trump opening 16-19 points. If you are in any doubt about the strength of the 1nt hand then enquire of the opener's partner. If you Double a one no-trump opening then it is a Penalty Double which means business in as much as you hope to defeat the opposition contract and gain penalty bonus points.

Now let's move one place round the table. Your partner has opened 1nt and the player on your right has Doubled. You will be either concerned about the Double or not worried about the Double and your bid of any suit or a pass will confirm the level of your concern as follows:

- Holding 7 or more points you will be fairly relaxed about the Double and will pass. After all, your partner does have between 12 and 14 points so between you there are about half the number of total points.

- Holding 5 or 6 points you should be a little concerned about the Double of your partner's 1nt and should at least consider a rescue.

- Holding 4 points or less you should be very worried and should bid your best suit as a rescue. Some partnerships have a rescue arrangement whereby a Re-Double or a bid of 2c will give the 1nt opener the chance to get out of trouble. This rescue bid is sometimes called a 'wriggle' upon which I will comment again in chapter 14.

Let's now move to the next place round the table where you find your partner has Doubled a 1nt opening bid. Your partner will have a hand holding between 15-18 points and be fairly balanced. What has the player on your right hand side done about the Double?

- That player has either bid a suit or has redoubled or has bid 2c as a rescue bid. If that player has bid in this way then the reason will probably be the lack of points which should mean that you will have a few points in your hand. Don't forget there is a strong hand opposite so with 7 or more points yourself you and your partner could well have something on.

- That player on your right has passed. Why has that player passed? It can only be because that player is relaxed about the Double which normally indicates points and that you should now not be at all relaxed about the Double and should rescue your partner by bidding your best suit at the next level.

Doubling for Penalties.

North will open 1nt
East will Double

South is not particularly worried
about the Double so will pass.

West, with 2 points, is worried
about the Double and will rescue
partner by bidding best suit – 2c.

	N	♠	J107		
		♥	J87		
		♦	AJ82		
W		♣	KQ2		

♠	Q96		♠	A84
♥	932	Dealer	♥	AK10
♦	754	North	♦	KQ9
♣	9863		♣	J754

		♠	K532		E
		♥	Q654		
		♦	1063		
		♣	A10	S	

North will pass as will East and
South, with those 9 points contemplates 2nt but decides against
because of the strong hand at East.   Contract 2c by West.

Look what happens when the South and West hands are swapped.

North opens 1nt.   East Doubles.

Holding only 2 points South must
now rescue partner and will bid
best suit 2c.

West now has 9 points and is very
aware that partner across the way
has a strong hand and with 9
points in hand will bid 3nt.

	N	♠	J107		
		♥	J87		
		♦	AJ82		
W		♣	KQ2		

♠	K532		♠	A84
♥	Q654	Dealer	♥	AK10
♦	1063	North	♦	KQ9
♣	A10		♣	J754

		♠	Q96		E
		♥	932		
		♦	754		
		♣	9863	S	

West was not too worried about
the Club bid by South. It was likely a rescue bid and after doing
some counting, calculated that South could not have more than two
or three points. North had 12-14 to open 1nt, East has 16 or so points
and West has 9 points, so adding those together and taking the total
from 40 leaves South with about 2 points.

Several months ago, one of my regular partners, a charming lady from Galway, politely whispered one of my habits at the Bridge table. Me, having a habit!! Apparently on occasions I used to show indecisiveness when selecting a bid from the bidding box.

So no more fiddling with the bidding cards before making a final choice as to what to bid but now I have another problem raised by the head of catering and laundry and the person who seems to play Bridge only to keep the peace with the head of car cleaning and heavy gardening. I do get the impression quite often that if I were to put forward to Margaret the idea that we do not play Bridge but sit in comfortable chairs in the lounge with friends and chat, that would be a very welcome suggestion. Put another way I don't think Margaret would object too much and after all we could all talk about forthcoming holidays, the grand-children and Rosemary's daughter's wedding plans.

Don't believe a word of it, but it is said that I mutter under my breath when considering the Dummy hand when first placed on the table and with respect to Margaret it seems the indistinct muttering is evident not necessarily when I play with Margaret which could, of course, give me a good reason for such murmurs. I do sometimes have to be a very patient partner when playing opposite the light of my life and if I do occasionally fidget and utter sounds under my breath then who can blame me?

At least I don't slowly wave a hand back and forth like a silk scarf blowing in the breeze when considering the Dummy hand and the tricks that could be made but I can tell you, from very recent experience, that I do on occasions have what is commonly called a mental block and these so called blocks seem to be occurring more and more these days. What happened? I'll tell you what happened.

I opened 1h with my 15 point hand, the LHO passed and my partner bid stop 3h. The 3h jump bid triggered sheer excitement in the mind of yours truly and he had visions of a slam looming which made him oblivious to anything else whilst concentrating on his partner's replies to the Ace seeking convention. I settled on 5h.

115

The hand my partner Sheila put down as Dummy contained nothing that should have caused me to go Ace hunting but I did not realise that at the time, which I later found very worrying. I thanked Sheila but it wasn't until I had played out the hands and only achieved 9 tricks and asked Sheila why she had jumped with only 11 points and received her reply in a very polite manner that it suddenly came home to me that the person who is writing a second book on Bridge had had a problem upstairs and that problem was fuzziness.

I had mistaken Sheila's jump bid in my opening suit as a jump in another suit which would have indicated a strong hand hence my Ace seeking exercise.

I am sure the reason for the failure in properly reading my partner's bid had a lot to with the situation at Bognor Regis railway station yesterday morning and which caused me to end up with a woolly brain last evening. I often cycle along the coast to or from Bognor Regis and the to or from aspect is whether I catch the train there or back dependent upon which way the wind is blowing. Normally I only cycle one way because Bognor is about ten miles away. Yesterday morning I cycled to Bognor along the coast and to my dismay there was a severe disruption with the train service so I turned heal and cycled home. I was exhausted.

Don't know what to do with the £2.85 I saved by not buying a rail ticket. I know, I'll buy one of those pens that I can hang round my neck for when I am interested in a telephone number given out by the radio or television. Most normal people, and in that category I include myself being particularly normal, would need to raise themselves from their easy chair and look for that pen which was in that drawer yesterday and is nowhere to be seen today. Having found a pen or pencil they would need to find their reading glasses and then something upon which to write and all that is to be accomplished in less than 2 seconds and then there's the question of the memory. And talking about memory – I must remember that when my partner jumps in my opening suit she may only have 10 points.

This set of hands show a double for take-out and a Re-Double

The Bidding -
East passes. South bids 1s.
West Doubles.
North Re-Doubles.
East bids 2h. South bids 2s
West passes
North bids 3s.
East passes then all pass.

Following East's pass, South will
open 1s. West also has a near
opening hand and not much in
the way of Spades bids a Double asking partner to bid best suit.

	N	♠	J62		
		♥	A52		
		♦	10974		
W		♣	AJ5		
♠	108			♠	K43
♥	QJ104		Dealer	♥	9873
♦	AQ8		East	♦	J63
♣	K1082			♣	764
		♠	AQ975		E
		♥	K6		
		♦	K52		
		♣	Q93	S	

Had it not been for the Double, North would have responded 1nt but after the Double, North will now show partner about 10 points and no more than 3 cards in partner's Spade suit, by a Re-Double.

East will answer partner's Double and bid 2h.

South will rebid 2s. West now has to contemplate the situation. There are opening points in front at South and about 10 points behind at North and 11 points in hand so partner opposite must have a very poor hand. The chances of success are poor so West wisely passes.

North has already shown about 10 points and can now confirm a fit in Spades with three in hand knowing there are at least five Spades opposite because partner has bid Spades twice. North bids 3s. East passes and South will also pass and leave the contract at 3s in view of the points in the West hand.

After seeing Partner's Dummy hand, South can calculate to a point or two the weakness of the East hand and capitalise on a finesse or two in the Dummy hand.

West will lead Q♥ hoping to promote the Jack and 10.

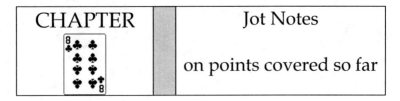

CHAPTER	Jot Notes
	on points covered so far

Opening 1nt + Responding with a Balanced Hand	Open 1nt with 12-14 points (no void, no singleton, no 2 doubletons, no 5 card major) Partner also balanced holding less than 11 points will PASS

The Responses holding 11 -12 points

Transfers NOT agreed		Transfers AGREED
2nt will show 11 or 12 points		2s to show exactly 11 points 2nt to show exactly 12 points

Holding 13 – 18 points then bid 3nt straight away

BUT

If you have a four card major then consider STAYMAN 2c
Opener will reply

2d	No four card major held
2h	4 Hearts held (4 Spades may also be held)
2s	4 Spades held (4 Hearts are not held)

After opener's reply to Stayman enquiry

Holding 11/12 points
No fit then bid 2nt
Fit then bid major at 3 level

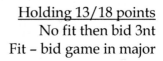

Holding 13/18 points
No fit then bid 3nt
Fit – bid game in major

A note for the opener holding 4 cards in both majors.
If your partner has bid 2c Stayman and you have replied 2h
and your partner then bids 2nt or 3nt,
your partner will be holding 4 Spades.

| Responding to Partner's 1nt holding an Unbalanced Hand | You are unbalanced because your hand contains a void of a suit, a singleton or two doubletons. |

Unbalanced and holding less than 11 points

Transfers NOT agreed		Transfers AGREED
Bid longest suit at 2 level but not Clubs unless significant - see note below		Holding five card major Bid 2d – partner will bid 2h. Bid 2h – partner will bid 2s.

If Clubs are significant bid Stayman 2c and then reply 3c.
If Diamonds, bid 2c and reply 3d but pass if negative 2d reply.

If you have 11/12 points and length in a minor.
Bid at the 3 level and leave the rest to your partner.
With 13 or more points and length in a minor bid 3nt.

If you have 11/18 points and length in a major bid at 3 level and
leave your partner to decide on game in the major or 3nt.
You may like to bid Stayman first.

With length in both majors and a negative reply after Stayman
bid 3d which is Extended Stayman asking for best 3 card major.

Still use the Transfer Convention holding 11 or more points.
After bidding 2d for transfer to Hearts or
After bidding 2h for transfer to Spades.

You bid 2nt showing 5 of major and 11/12 points
You bid 3nt showing 5 of major and 13 or more points.
You will give partner double the information in just 1 bid.

With 13 or more points and length in a minor bid 3nt.

Opening at 1 level + Responses with 0-10 points.	Open at 1 level with 10-19 points. If you only have 10/11 points you will have either a 6 card suit or two 5 card suits or you have considered the Rule of 20.

Open longest suit
Length before Strength - Quantity before Quality.

With 2 x 5 card suits open higher except two black suits.
With 2x4 card biddable suits open the higher except 2 black suits.

With 4441
If one suit is not biddable then treat as a two suiter.
Otherwise if singleton is red open biddable suit below
and if singleton is black then open the middle of the other 3 suits.

Responding to partner's unopposed opening 1 level bid.

Holding less than 6 points – you PASS
Exception and with agreement of partner
Holding only 5 points but support for major, bid at 2 level.

Holding 6/7 points.
Bid 4 card major at 1 level over partner's minor opening.
Do not support partner's minor before showing your 4 card major.
With both majors bid the Hearts first.
Otherwise support partner's minor at 2 level.

Holding 8/10 points *(in some partnerships the range is 9/10)*
Still show your major over partner's minor at the 1 level.
Support your partner's suit at the 2 level or
Bid your own 5 or more card suit at the 2 level.
Supporting major – consider Losing Trick Count (next page)

Holding 6/10 points and not a suit to bid

You need 8 points *(9/10 in some partnerships)* and a five card suit to change the suit and bid at the 2 level. If you cannot bid a suit at the 2 level then bid 1nt and your hand does not need to be balanced.

You must have five Hearts to bid 2h after partner's 1s opening.

Opener's Rebid - under 15 points Losing Trick Count Adding Distribution Points	Holding less than 15 points you will have a weak opening hand.

Four things you **must not do** holding a weak opening hand
a). Rebid above the 2 level in your opening suit.
b). Rebid a suit in sequence, above that of your first bid suit.
c). Jump in partner's suit.
d). Get excited when partner supports.   One up – shut up.

Four things **you can do** holding a weak opening hand.
a). Rebid your opening suit at the 2 level to confirm five cards.
b). Bid another suit, (at least 4 cards) lower in sequence than the first.
c). Support your partner's suit at the next level holding four cards.
d). Remember one up – shut up when partner supports your suit.

The Losing Trick Count - When able to support your partner's major
1 level opening bid when distribution counts as much as points.

Void or Singleton Ace – No losers.
Any other singleton or Ax or Kx – 1 loser.
Any other doubleton – 2 losers.
With AJ10 count as – 1 loser
With Qxx and partner not bid suit – 3 losers
Any other 3 card suit without A,K or Q – 3 losers.
Deduct 1 loser for each trump over four cards held in hand.

Assume 7 losers in opener's hand and add your losers and then
deduct from 18 and whatever the answer bid at that level. If the
answer is 5 then bid to game not at the 5 level. If you are vulnerable
and your hand looks somewhat ropey then temper your reply.

Adding points for Distribution
In long trump hand – void = 4 points and singleton = 2 points.
In short trump hand – void = 5 points and singleton = 3 points.
A doubleton in the short trump hand = 1 point.

The Simple Overcall
No-Trump Overcall
Responding to Overcall
The Jump Overcall

To overcall in a suit
you <u>must have</u> at least <u>five cards</u>
in the overcall suit.

To overcall at the <u>1 level</u> you need 8-15 points
To overcall at the <u>2 level</u> you need 10-15 points
To overcall at the <u>3 level</u> you need 12-15 points.

To overcall 1nt you must have at least 15 points and a stop or two in the opener's suit.

I must stress again that in some partnerships the minimum number of points for overcalling at the one level is 9. Your must discuss this with your partner and agree what level. Some partnerships I know do not overcall at the one level unless they have at least 10 points but I consider this rather restrictive.

If partner has overcalled in a suit you can support with only 3 cards. Holding 0-4 points best you pass. Also pass with 5-9 points unless you can support. Holding 10+ points try and find a bid be it no-trumps or your own five card suit. With support for partner avoid going off on your own unless your suit is strong.

If your partner has overcalled 1nt then you know partner has at least 15 points and must have a stop or two in the opener's suit. With 8 points bid an invitational 2nt or with 9 or more points then bid 3nt.

If you are in the fourth position and your partner has overcalled and you have stops in the opening bid suit plus 10 points then bid the opener's suit. Your partner will alert and bid own suit again if at the lower end of the overcall point range or bid another suit if higher which may provide encouragement for a game in no-trumps.

With a strong hand (15+ points) and six cards in suit then jump overcall. After an opening bid of say 1d you would jump overcall and bid stop 2h.

The Doubles

<u>The opposition have bid at the 1 level in a suit.</u>
You have an opening or near opening hand. You have a shortage in the bid suit. You will have quality cards in the other three suits. The Double asks partner to bid best suit, which becomes discretional if opener's partner bids. With 8 or less losers partner will consider jumping.

<u>Two suits bid by opposition and partner passed.</u>
Sitting fourth position, tells partner you have the other two suits.

<u>After suit opening by partner and RHO has bid.</u>
Tells partner that hand is weak and bidding space been stolen.
Your partner bids say 1d. RHO bids 1s and you wanted to bid 1h.

<u>After suit opening by partner and RHO has bid.</u>
Bidding space not stolen but holding four spades and quite weak such as 1d opening by partner, 1h by RHO. Your Double shows a weak hand but holding 4 Spades.

> CARE - If your partner has Doubled for take-out and there are no further bids then that Take-Out Double will convert to a Penalty Double.

<u>Penalty Double after opposition 1nt bid</u>

The doubler will have 15-18 points.
Opener's partner will rescue holding less than 7 points.
Doubler's partner will rescue with low points if RHO passes.
Doubler's partner will bid 2nt with 7/8 points.
Doubler's partner will bid to 3nt with 9 or more points.

The Seven Young Ladies of Arun

At the Bridge Club you will occasionally come across grumpy men and grouchy women who are there only for the Bridge and to win and there are those who are there just to enjoy a pleasant interlude and it is those folk who make life at the club so pleasurable and where winning is not the be-all and end-all.

At my local Bridge club there is a group of ladies who regularly partner each other with whom I can always have lots of friendly banter. There's Wendy, Maureen, Terry, Jean, Jan, another Wendy and another Maureen.   These ladies are all of a similar standard and some while ago they all attended four refresher sessions with me to perk up their game. Many bids they make are with some hesitation and their climb up the 'spiral staircase' to a game bid is often with an element of indecision which on two occasions recently, lulled me into a false sense of security. The first occasion was their bid of 5d and the second was their bid of 5h and on both occasions the Declarer was named Wendy, the taller of the two ladies with that name and the only lady, to date, in the 'Arun Seven' to have purchased my first book.

On the two occasions in question the body language of the two ladies when bidding to their game contracts gave me the distinct impression that they were not going to succeed and on both occasions I fell into the trap and Doubled only to give them bonus points and a great deal of satisfaction when their coach failed in his attempt to defeat. Much laughter ensued and each time I said I was never again going to take notice of any of these ladies' hesitation.

However up the spiral staircase to 5h went one Wendy and one Maureen last night and one Bryan, whilst giving Wendy a knowing glance, Doubled, being very mindful of the history. Fortunately, with much relief, my Double bore fruit in the shape of 800 points.

As well as Bridge, the ladies play golf and by the way they all relate to one another they must have a great deal of fun when they are together. It's good to see and it is people like them that make our local club a good place to go on Mondays and Fridays.

CHAPTER 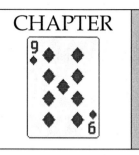	Opener's Rebid – 15 points + Partner Supports Opening Bid Reverse No- Trump The Jump Shift The Suit Reverse Supporting Partner's Bid

The Nine of Diamonds is called the Curse of Scotland. As there appears to be several reasons for the description I will leave you to investigate yourself if you are interested. I did start to explain but found I got myself bogged down and in any event my mind was on other things. To be honest it was 'my chair'. It wasn't a case of who's been sitting in my chair, I knew the culprit having caught her in the act and it wasn't Goldilocks either. Why do I like to sit in my lounge in one particular chair? I gave the same answer as I did to the question last year as to why did I need to buy a sports car which would spend most if its time in the garage. Because I do.

What are we doing now? Oh yes – opener's rebid with a strong hand.

Everybody else bar me calls it the Suit Reverse,
which is the proper name
but I give it a clearer description

Jumping over the Boundary Fence
but more on that later

Earlier I dealt with weak 1 level opening hands in a suit with a point range of 10-14 and where you showed the weak opening hand on your rebid. This chapter is going to deal with strong 1 level suit opening hands containing 15-17 points and very strong 1 level opening hands containing 18 or 19 points.

Holding 10-19 points you open the bidding in the normal way in a suit and on your rebid you confirm the strength of your hand. Holding a weak opening hand you confirm that weakness by re-bidding your opening suit at the next level or bidding another suit in a lower sequence than your opening bid suit.

In this chapter, on your rebid you will be confirming a strong or very strong hand by one of five methods

1. Your rebid after your partner supports your opening bid.

2. Reversing into no-trumps.

3. A suit reverse (jumping over your first suit fence).

4. Jumping in your first bid suit.

5. Jumping in partner's suit.

Your partner supports your opening bid. – If you have a weak opening hand with up to 14 points and your partner supports your opening suit then it is usually a case of <u>one-up, shut-up</u>. However if you have 15, 16 or 17 points invite game in a major by bidding at the 3 level inviting partner to bid to game if partner has high points in the range promised, or if you have 18 or 19 points and your partner supports your major then bid straight to game in your major. If your partner supports your opening bid in a minor then consider the Reverse No-trump discussed next or the Suit Reverse discussed on page 129.

Reversing into no-trumps – You have a fairly balanced opening hand with between 15-19 points and thus too strong to open 1nt. You will therefore bid a suit with the intention of reversing into no-trumps on your rebid depending on what your partner says. Alternatively you have an unbalanced hand but the response by your partner corrects any imbalance. For example you may have a Roman hand 4441 and your partner bids your singleton suit.

If your partner responds at the 1 level in a suit you cannot support with four cards, particularly a major, you will rebid:

1nt holding 15/16 points
2nt holding 17/18 points or
3nt holding exactly 19 points.

If your partner responds at the 2 level in a suit you cannot support with four cards you will rebid 2nt holding 15/16 points and 3nt holding 17/19 points. The responder would have shown at least 8 points (9 points in some partnerships) by changing the suit and bidding at the 2 level so a 2nt rebid by opener must therefore show only 15/16 points. With more points, game would have been bid.

If after your reverse into 1nt showing 15/16 points, your partner bids 2nt, your partner will have exactly 9 points in hand. Stands to reason. Partner would have passed with less than 9 points because no chance of reaching game points even with your maximum 16, and your partner would have bid straight to game with more than 9 points. Your minimum 15 points + 10 or more points.

Have a look at the hands that follow which will show all these aspects of the reverse no-trump showing a strong hand.

Opener				Responder
Opens 1d	K85	♠	Q96	1h
	J93	♥	K1064	
Rebid 1nt	AK85	♦	Q4	3nt.
	AJ8	♣	K972	

Open 1d – (too strong to open 1nt). Responder can bid at the 1 level with only 4 cards. Would need 5 cards to change suit and bid at 2 level. Opener's rebid of 1nt is the reverse no-trump showing 15/16 points. Responder knows partner has at least 15 points so with 10 in hand will bid to game.

Opener				Responder
Opens 1d	K85	♠	962	2c
	J93	♥	K106	
Rebid 2nt	AK85	♦	Q4	pass
	AJ8	♣	K9732	

Same opening hand as above but now the response is 2c which is a change of suit showing at least 5 clubs & 8 points. Opener cannot now reverse into 1nt showing 15/16 points but now has to bid 2nt. Responder knows that the 2nt bid is only showing 15/16 points because having shown at least 8 points in hand, opener with 17/18 points would have bid straight to game.

Opener				Responder
Opens 1c	Q85	♠	A74	1h
	J93	♥	AJ54	
1nt	AK8	♦	9732	2nt
	AJ85	♣	93	
Pass				

Opener is too strong to open 1nt and thus bids 1c and after partner's response of 1h, reverses into no-trumps and bids 1nt showing a window of 15/16 points. Responder has exactly 9 points and invites partner by bidding 2nt. The opener now knows that responder has exactly 9 points because with less than 9 points partner would have passed and with more than 9 points would have bid straight to game. Opener with the lower of the 15/16 promised will decline the invitation and pass.

Opener				Responder
1h	K7	♠	9852	1s
	QJ842	♥	93	
Stop 2nt	AK7	♦	Q93	3nt
	KJ5	♣	AQ83	

After partner's 1s response confirming at least 6 points and 4 Spades, the opener confirms 17/18 points by bidding – stop 2nt. The responder with those 8 points knows there are at least 17 points opposite and bids to game – 3nt.

Opener				Responder
1h	K7	♠	A63	1nt
	QJ842	♥	A9	
2nt	AK7	♦	J863	3nt
	KJ5	♣	9864	

This time the opener does not need to reverse into no-trumps because partner has responded 1nt showing 6-10 points. The opener's rebid of 2nt is invitational and invites game if partner holds points in the higher end of the 6-10 range already shown. With 9 points the responder bids to game.

Opener				Responder
1d	AQ7	♠	J943	1s
	AK8	♥	J94	
Stop – 3nt	K865	♦	A7	pass
	QJ3	♣	9874	

With the sure knowledge that there are at least six points opposite then holding exactly 19 points, the opener reverses into no-trumps and bids – stop 3nt. Whilst only having promised at least six points, the responder knows there are exactly 19 points in partner's hand and with that knowledge can respond accordingly. In this case, holding only 6 points the responder passes.

The Suit Reverse. This time you can show your partner your strong hand on your rebid by a suit reverse. I refer to it as **Jumping over your first suit fence**. I'll explain what I mean.

Open 1c the fence is 2c, open 1d and the fence is 2d, 1h and the fence is 2h and so on. If you open at the 1 level in a suit and your rebid, guaranteeing only 4 cards in another suit, is at a level the other side of the fence then you will have shown a strong hand – 15/19 points. A common shape for a reverse bid is 5/4 showing the 5 card suit first.

You open in the normal way in a suit at the 1 level and your rebid, holding a strong hand, is at the next level in a higher sequence suit. For example, if opened 1c and your partner bid 1h and your second biddable suit was Diamonds, you would rebid 2d. How would your partner know you had a strong hand? You opened 1c, the fence was 2c and your rebid was the other side of the fence – 2d.

Look at the following examples where you would be jumping over your first suit fence to show a strong opening hand.

Opening bid 1h – rebid 2s or 3c or 3d.
Opening bid 1d – rebid 2h or 2s or 3c.
Opening bid 1s – rebid 3c, 3d or 3h.
Opening bid 1c – rebid 2d, 2h, 2s

Opener				Responder
1d	9	♠	AQ2	2c
	AJ65	♥	J85	
2h	AK753	♦	96	stop 3nt
	KJ6	♣	Q9842	

Length before strength, opener bids 1d and after partner's 2c response, will rebid 2h showing not only the second suit but also a strong hand. The opening bid was 1d so the first bid suit fence is 2d. The rebid of 2h is the other side of the 2d fence. The responder knows that there is a strong hand opposite and two suits covered. With game points and the Spades stopped, will bid to game in no-trumps – stop 3nt.

Opener				Responder
1h	AQ85	♠	963	2c
	KJ752	♥	Q93	
stop 2s	AQ92	♦	K8	stop 4h
	void	♣	A9765	
pass				

Opener started with 5 card heart suit and after partner's 2c response, the strong hand and the second suit was shown and the reverse also confirmed the very likely presence of 5 cards in the first bid suit. Therefore the responder with 9 points and three Heart cards to make the fit is relaxed at bidding game - 4h.

NOTICE

YOU MUST BE
15 OR OVER TO
JUMP THIS
FENCE

This very faithful dog called Karla was a great mate of mine. She was a rescue and soon became very much part of our family. The notice on the fence reads 'YOU MUST BE 15 OR OVER TO JUMP THIS FENCE'. I've set up this picture to bring home the necessity for at least 15 points to show your partner a strong opening hand.

If your hand is fairly balanced, try and show the strength by a reverse no-trump by a rebid of 1nt with 15/16, 2nt with 17/18 and 3nt with exactly 19 points. With an unbalanced strong hand show your second suit after jumping over your first suit fence.

The Jump Shift – Simple enough and best when holding a major suit. After your partner has responded to your 1 level suit opening bid, you jump in your opening suit to the 3 level. So 1h – 1s – stop 3h confirms at least a six card suit and a strong hand. Then partner with the balance of points and only two cards in the suit to make the fit, bids to game as in this example.

Opener				Responder
1h	J5	♠	A642	1s
	KQ9853	♥	107	
stop 3h	AQ5	♦	J9	4h
	A5	♣	KJ642	

Jumping in Partner's Suit – You open the bidding at the 1 level and your partner changes the suit and bids a major. With four card support for partner's major, bid at the next level holding a weak opening hand with 10-14 points, but jump a level holding a strong hand with 15-17 points and bid to game holding a very strong hand 18-19 points. Better explained by the illustration:

Your opening 1 level hand will contain 10 – 19 points		
A weak opening hand 10 – 14 points	A strong opening hand 15 – 17 points	A very strong opening hand 18 – 19 points
If you open at the 1 level and your partner bids a major, in which suit you have 4 cards, then support in accordance with your opening strength.		
10-14 rebid next level	15-17 jump one level	18-19 bid to game

By all means support your partner's minor suit but game is further away than in a major. It is often better to first explore a no trump contract rather than a game in a minor suit when 11 tricks have to be made. Game in a minor and making 11 tricks scores the same as making 9 tricks and game in no-trumps.

The following set of hands demonstrate the sense in exploring a no-trump contract rather than a minor contract when the opener has a strong hand and can support partner's response in a minor suit.

Don't ask your partner to make the decision when you can more easily make the decision yourself.

N	♠	Q876
	♥	J953
	♦	J
W	♣	KJ32

♠	A53			♠	KJ10
♥	62	Dealer		♥	AK87
♦	AQ985	East		♦	10732
♣	1095			♣	AQ

	♠	942	E
	♥	Q104	
	♦	K64	
	♣	8764	S

The Bidding
East opens 1h.
South passes
West bids 2d.
North passes.
East bids 3d **(WRONG)**
South passes.

What does West do now?
Why has East left the final decision to West who will most likely pass?

After East's 3d bid, West is left in the wilderness, not knowing what to do next. Why did East leave the decision to partner when the decision could have been made by East?

Don't ask your partner to make the decision when you can more easily make the decision yourself.

East had all the answers and should have bid 3nt straight away after the 2d bid by partner. After all the 2d bid guaranteed 8 points and with 17 in hand and the Clubs and the Spades not too badly covered there were enough points for game. Why invite game in a minor having to achieve 11 tricks when a better game is available in no-trumps when only 9 tricks are needed.

South will innocently lead the 7♣ (high non-honour confirming no interest in the suit) which will delight the Declarer holding that AQ doubleton in Clubs.

SHOWING YOUR PARTNER THE STRENGTH OF YOUR HAND
after partner bids another suit.

YOUR FIRST BID – Opening in a suit at the 1 level

You hold between 10 & 19 points.
(Holding 10/11 points you have a six card or two five card suits or you have opened using the Rule of 20)

Partner bids another suit you cannot support

YOUR SECOND BID –telling partner the strength of your hand.

10-14 points		15 – 19 points
You will bid another suit at the 1 level. 1d – 1h – 1s or You will bid opening suit at the 2 level. 1d – 1s – 2d or You will bid another suit in a lower sequence than your first suit at the 2 level which will normally confirm five cards in your first bid suit. 1h – 1s – 2c CARE If you reverse into no-trumps or bid another suit in a higher sequence to your first bid suit, you will be showing your partner <u>more than 14 points</u>.		Reverse into no-trumps with a balanced hand or after partner's bid has satisfied a shortage. 1d – 1s – 1nt holding 15/16 1c – 1h – stop 2nt holding 17/18 1d – 1h – stop 3nt holding 19 1h – 2c – 2nt holding 15/16 OR You jump over your boundary fence or as correctly termed you reverse in suit. 1d – 1s – 2h (fence was 2d) 1h – 1s – stop 3c (fence was 2h) OR You jump bid in your opening suit holding six cards in the suit. 1h – 2c – stop 3h. 1s – 2d – stop 3s.

SHOWING YOUR PARTNER THE STRENGTH OF YOUR HAND
When you can support your partner's response suit

You open the bidding <u>but your partner responds in your second suit</u>. The following is best done when your partner responds in a major suit but if partner responds in a minor, being your second suit then try for no-trumps first.

Opener's Points

10 – 14	15-16-17	18-19
In this sector just bid at the next level. 1d – 1s – 2s 1c – 1h – 2h	In this sector jump one level 1d – 1s –stop 3s 1c – 1h – stop 3h	In this sector jump two levels 1d – 1s – stop 4s 1c – 1h – stop 4h.

If you rebid correctly your partner will know your points sector enabling your partner to bid according to the points held in hand.

SHOWING YOUR PARTNER THE STRENGTH OF YOUR HAND
When partner supports your opening suit straight away.

10 – 14 points	15,16,17 points	18,19 points
Or poor 15 point hand Just pass. One up-shut up 1h -2h – pass 1c – 2c - pass	With good looking 15 points or 16/17 points invite game in a major by bidding at the 3 level. Or With balanced hand consider a reverse no-trump. Remember your partner may have 8,9 or 10 points or perhaps only 6 or 7.	Bid to game in a major but investigate no-trumps with support in your minor before considering game in the minor Or Consider reversing into 2nt with 17/18 or 3nt holding exactly 19.

In a book like this I know you would expect some reference to Greek Mythology so here we go and whilst at it some reference to the Sputnik double.

Playing Bridge you do need to expect the unexpected. Things may not turn out the way you expect. I'm going to mention Hermes in a second but first of all you must never take for granted what may appear to be obvious. Just suppose you have successfully finessed and won a trick in Dummy with the Queen, holding AQ, being convinced the King was in the hand before and not played because of your Dummy's Ace sitting beyond. So frustrated you will be when playing the suit again to find the King was in fact sitting behind the Dummy's Queen and not played and then you cannot get into the Dummy hand with all the remaining winners hence the reason the King was not played after your Queen. Clever defenders.

The month of May has come upon us. The name of May was probably after the Roman goddess Maia, who in Ancient Greek mythology was the mother of Hermes. Not having had a classical education I am going to look up this chappie Hermes.

Hermes otherwise known as Mercurius by the Romans, was one of the Greek gods and was the son of Zeus. His birthplace is of no consequence but fancy having a father like Zeus. As the story goes, he ate his pregnant first wife, Metis, goddess of Wisdom, fearing their child Athena would be greater than himself. Seems the sex of the unborn was attainable even then. Eating his wife did not affect the birth because the child later sprung, fully armed, from Zeus' head when Hephaestus, whoever he was, split it with an axe. See what I mean by expecting the unexpected.

It says, according to the legends, this chap Hermes had only been born a few hours when he stole the cattle of his brother Apollo which he drove from Pieria to Pylos presumably still wearing a wet nappy. Before that he invented the lyre leaving before nightfall to rustle the immortal cattle of his brother. What good fortune it was that Hermes had invented and had crudely manufactured the lyre on the first day of his life, by stringing an empty tortoise shell with cow gut, because when Apollo found out about the cattle an argument ensued, quite naturally, but Hermes' playing of the instrument enchanted Apollo to such an extent that he agreed that Hermes retain the stolen cattle in exchange for the lyre.

It gets more interesting by the second just like being the Declarer when some Dummy hands go down on the table. This chap Hermes was the god of Prudence and Cunning and as such he was worshipped by merchants and traders and his reputation for ingenuity caused him to be regarded, for some reason I cannot as yet imagine, as the author of the alphabet, numbers, weights and measures. He was also worshipped as the patron of roads and travellers and was also the God of luck and dice games

I wonder what he did on the third day of his life. Probably had sex with Penelope and fathered Pan and in the afternoon went out on his chariot meeting Chione on the way causing the birth of Autolycus the Thief. Did he, on the fourth day of his life - steel the crown jewels?

Talking about stealing. You are holding 6-10 points and four Hearts. Your partner opens 1c or 1d and you immediately know that your response is going to be 1h but that person on your right hand side bids 1s which stops you in your tracks. The person sitting on your right has stolen your bidding space. You are too weak to bid 2h so what do you do? You Double. The Double is not a penalty double, it is a take-out Double telling your partner that you would have bid 1h had it not been for the 1s bid by the opposition and that you are too weak to bid 2h.

CHAPTER	Responding to a 1 level Opening Bid with 11 or more points + Delayed Game Raise

When you hold less than 11 points you need 5 cards and 8 points (some partnerships require 9) if you respond to your partner's 1 level bid by bidding another suit. If you have 11 or more points you do not need the qualification of five cards to bid another suit and you are able to bid another suit holding only four cards. However, you will by now come to expect an exception.

If you bid 2h after your partner's 1s opening then your partner will

♠	J5
♥	A953
♦	Q975
♣	AJ8

expect you to have at least five Heart cards irrespective of the number of points held. The reason for this is that a fit in Hearts is found easily by the opener holding only three Heart cards. Your response holding this hand would be 2d. Strange though because you will be denying a four card major.

With 11 or more points in hand and your partner has opened, the chances of a game in a suit or in no-trumps are quite high so your response to your partner who has opened should not indicate that you are weak.

With 11 or more points
Do not bid a suit at the 2 level after a 1nt opening (a weak take-out) except when bidding 2c Stayman asking for a reply.

Do not support your partner at the 2 level except when losing trick count dictates otherwise (one up – shut up).

Do not bid 1nt after your partner's opening in a suit. If you do not have a suit to bid then bid 2nt which will indicate your not having a suit to bid and 11/12 points.

All the 'do not' bids would indicate weakness but with 11 or more points you are <u>not weak</u>. Endeavour to find a suit to reach game or game in no-trumps but holding only 11/12 points always be mindful of the fact that your partner may also have a similar number of points or even less. Your partner may have opened with two five card suits or a six card suit with only 10 HCP's in hand.

With 11 (+) points and support for your partner's major opening, do the Losing Trick Count just as you do with less than 11 points. If you cannot support your partner's suit, bid another suit to see what your partner says next and that will be one of the following:

> Your partner who opened will confirm a weak opening
> hand with 10/14 points by a:

- Bid of the first suit again at the 2 level showing five cards in that suit. Would not have another biddable suit of 4 cards.
- Bid of a suit in a lower sequence than the first at the 2 level. This will normally confirm five cards in the first bid suit and at least four cards in the second suit.

or your partner who opened will confirm more than 14 points by:

- A suit reverse (jumping the first suit fence) and bidding a second suit at a higher level than the first bid suit.
- Reversing into no-trumps. 1nt=15/16, 2nt=17/18 & 3nt=19.
- Jump shift – jumping on first bid suit.
- Jump in your suit.

If your partner has opened the bidding at the one level and you have 11/12 points but no biddable four or five card suit then bid - stop 2nt leaving partner to decide what to do. Your partner may pass with only 12 points but bid to game with 14 points or good 13 points.

Whatever you do, try and indicate to your partner that you have 11 or more points and with 13 or more points always do your best to reach a game contract.

	N		
	♠	KQ873	
	♥	K62	
	♦	AJ10	
W	♣	J9	

♠	J9			♠	654
♥	743		Dealer	♥	QJ1095
♦	8754		North	♦	32
♣	AKQ10			♣	765

	♠	A102	E
	♥	A8	
	♦	KQ96	
	♣	8432	S

North bids 1s and East passes. South has only four Diamonds but having 11 or more points can now bid the four card suit (unlike the situation when having less than 11 points) knowing that North will bid again when South will be able to decide what to do next.

West passes.

North will rebid 2s to show those 5 Spades and a <u>weak opening hand</u> of less than 15 points. North does <u>not</u> have a strong hand so should <u>not rebid</u> showing a hand in any of the following four categories.

- Jumping over first suit fence – the suit reverse.
- A jump shift – jumping in first bid suit.
- The reverse no-trump–1nt 15/16, 2nt 17/18, 3nt 19 points
- Jumping in partner's responding suit.

East passes.

South now knows for sure that partner has at least five Spades having bid them twice and also that partner does not have more than 14 points – a weak opening hand in fact. With three Spades in hand, a fit has been found and with 13 points in hand South can jump straight to game and bid 4s.

North opens 1s and East passes.

	N	♠	KQ873		
		♥	KJ62		
		♦	QJ		
		♣	J4		

South has 11 or more points so can therefore bid a different suit holding only four cards. With less than 11 points South would have needed five cards to bid another suit at the 2 level. South responds 2c, the lower of the two biddable minors

W					E
♠	AJ9			♠	1065
♥	A3	Dealer		♥	Q1095
♦	8754	North		♦	1032
♣	10832			♣	Q76

	♠	42
	♥	874
	♦	AK96
	♣	AK95	S

West will pass.

North bids 2h which will show partner three things.

- Holding 5 Spades – having rebid a second suit in a lower suit sequence at the two level.
- Holding at least four Hearts.
- Holding a weak opening hand – 14 points or less.

East will pass.

South has enough points for game and as partner has confirmed the three aspects of hand as outlined above then with the other two suits covered will bid stop 3nt.

It is very important that the opener's rebid shows the strength of the opening hand. As opener, tell your partner your strength otherwise how will your partner know?

It is so important that the 'conversation' you have with your partner is as informative as possible. The whole point of bidding is to give your partner information about your hand and the number of points in hand is something of great interest especially if your partner has got more than a few points. Tell your partner about your points on your rebid.

There are three bids on each line below. The first is the opening bid, the second is the responder bid and the third is the opener's rebid. There have not been any bids by the opposition. The column on the right side shows the point count of the opening hand.

Opening bid	Response	Opener's Rebid	Opener's strength	Opener's points
1h	1s	2c	weak	10-14
1s	2c	2s	weak	10-14
1d	1s	2h	strong	15-19
1h	1s	3h	strong	15-19
1c	1s	3s	strong	15-17
1h	2d	2nt	strong	15-16
1d	1h	2nt	strong	17-18
1c	1d	1nt	strong	15-16
1d	1s	2c	weak	10-14
1d	1h	3nt	very strong	19
1h	1nt	2h	weak	10-14
1s	2h	3d	strong	15-19
1d	1h	2h	weak	10-14
1s	2h	4h	strong	18-19
1s	2h	3c	strong	15-19
1d	1h	2c	weak	10-14
1d	1h	2s	strong	15-19

The Delayed Game Raise

As responder, after your partner has opened at the 1 level in a suit you will be holding 15 or more points and you know for a fact that game is a certainly barring Murphy's Law. You have two options.

- You tell your partner straight away by jumping into another suit such as 1d – stop 2h or 1h – stop 3c or
- <u>You delay telling your partner about your strong hand</u> until after you have had your partner's rebid which will be most informative indicating a weak or a strong opening hand as discussed earlier. You just bid normally and change the suit so your partner will definitely bid again.

I favour the second option, <u>The Delayed Game Raise</u>, because if you tell your partner straight away about your big hand you take up a lot of bidding space and you may cause the partnership to miss out on a slam bid. No damage is normally done by the delay in telling your partner about your strong hand so long as you do not make a bid which your partner could pass.

What not to do if your partner has opened the bidding at the 1 level in a suit and you have a strong hand.

Do not bid your partner's suit at the 2 level because your partner will think you are weak and may pass. One up-shut up.

Do not bid 1nt because it is not a forcing bid and your partner could pass because you are confirming a 6 – 10 point hand.

Do not bid 2nt because you will be telling your partner about only 11 or 12 points and with only 12 points in hand your partner will pass.

Do not bid your own strong suit at game level because your partner may interpret the bid as a 'shut out' and pass. Your partner may have a strong hand and you may miss a little slam or even that lovely Grand Slam.

This is a situation where your partner has opened the bidding at the 1 level in a suit, your RHO has passed and you delay showing your strong hand until partner has rebid.

N	♠	KJ9
	♥	J
	♦	A1094
W	♣	AK842

♠	1087		♠	5432
♥	1075	Dealer	♥	98432
♦	8632	North	♦	KJ
♣	J97		♣	Q3

	♠	AQ6	E
	♥	AKQ6	
	♦	Q75	
	♣	1065	S

The Bidding
North opens 1c
East passes.
South bids 1h.
West passes.
North rebids 2d.
East passes.
South then embarks on an Ace and King seeking exercise to reach a slam.

Notice that South, very much aware that game is a certainly, delays showing a strong hand because North may also have a strong hand which will not be shown until North's rebid. North indeed does have a strong hand and will show that strength by bidding over the other side of the Club fence – 2d.

South now knows the slam prospects having 17 points in hand and about 16 points opposite and bids in accordance with the agreed Ace and King seeking procedure – either Gerber or Blackwood discussed in chapter 16

....

A reminder of not what to do when delaying a game raise.

- Do not bid partner's suit at the 2 level because your partner, holding a weak opening hand, could pass.
- Do not bid 1nt or 2nt. Your partner could still pass.

It will be your fault if game is missed
because you took a chance that your partner would bid again.
With a strong hand change the suit and
MAKE YOUR PARTNER BID AGAIN.

The Telephone Call at Meal Times
With Respect - You know what I mean.

A friend of mine mentioned something specific to me and part way through the point he was making he confirmed he had mentioned it to Mark. Not having an inkling who Mark was and believing the name was relevant having been mentioned, on interrupting his specific point to enquire, I was told that Mark was the next door neighbour who had been so helpful during .... I can't remember what now but what I can remember is that I completely lost the gist of what my friend was trying to tell me in the first place, if you know what I mean?

I'm sure you do know what I mean when I mention that so many folk make a perfectly clear statement then immediately suffix it by – saying 'do you know I mean?' or 'do you understand what I am saying?' Some folk have the irritating, to me anyway, habit of saying 'do you know what I mean' after almost every third sentence and I wonder if it is the same folk who regularly say 'with respect'. With respect I do not think you have grasped the point and with respect I think you are talking a load of rubbish which is hardly respectful.

Just under an hour ago I sat down in my regular chair at the dining table for my evening meal which looked delicious. With respect it was boring, if you know what I mean, but it looked and was delicious. I've told Margaret to keep the 'boring meals' (her words) coming because they are always so appetising and what more could a chap like me want? For the previous fifteen minutes I had been in smelling distance of the kitchen and I eagerly awaited the call from you know who.

I took my first mouthful of the chicken casserole and the telephone rang. I sighed and arose from my seat very quickly for fear of Margaret rushing to answer the call. I knew the call would be for Margaret but being the 'white liar' in my house I am able to tell the caller that Margaret had not returned and was not expected back for a couple of hours or polite words to that effect. If Margaret manages to reach the telephone before me during an evening meal time, the caller's initial words will inevitably enquire whether Margaret is having her evening meal and if so she won't keep her long and please note the gender of the caller. Twenty minutes later, I've finished my meal without the pleasant company I prefer and then had to wait twiddling my fingers and watching sparrows going to and from the bird table and pigeons collecting all the seed droppings while Margaret finishes her meal and I am very sorry for not putting Margaret's meal in the warm oven while she was on the phone. So you see I do have to be on my guard at meal times and get to the telephone first when it rings.

It is always best to tell the caller that Margaret is absent because the 'only one minute' the caller promises to keep Margaret turns into ten or more and then the caller goes and has her lovely meal with her partner without any disturbance at all. I hope you are still taking note of the gender.

Whilst on the subject of the telephone I do get a little agitated when the person on the phone jumps the queue. Margaret wants something from the shops. I have changed my trousers because I cannot go down the town in 'those trousers', put on my shoes and outdoor coat. I've walked the half mile to the shop during which it started to pppp...pppp persistently rain. I'm in the shop having made quite an effort to be there with raindrops running down my cheeks and I wait my turn to be served. I'm finally at the counter, the shop keeper has politely enquired as to my requirements. I open my mouth to speak and the telephone rings. If I am really lucky I will get 'will you excuse me' and without waiting for an answer I am then ignored while the telephone is answered. I am then very annoyed because the caller is probably sitting at home, in his favourite chair, wearing 'those trousers', comfortable slippers and very warm.

There's me dripping wet and cold, heading for pneumonia having made all that effort and the person on the phone, with respect, takes priority, if you know what I mean.

Now back to the Bridge.

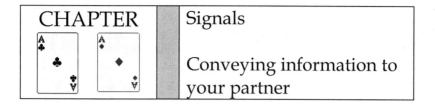

CHAPTER	Signals
	Conveying information to your partner

Signals - which are a poor substitute for logic.

Whilst you sit there in defence quietly hoping your partner will lead a particular suit because you have the Ace or the King or perhaps you hold the Queen when the Ace and King are in Dummy or that you want a particular suit led so that you can ruff, you can actually indicate your preferences to your partner by a method of signals.

There are several <u>permitted</u> signals and some signals which are most definitely <u>not permitted</u> but nevertheless have been tried. Touching partner's foot under the table, putting hand on your heart when you need a Heart lead and holding your fan of cards with fingers indicating the number of Aces held and scratching your face with fingers indicating the number of Kings held. Biting lip says something and scratching an armpit says something else. A false cough, touching a played card on the table and it goes on. Those who play regularly together can get away with all sorts of misdemeanours but fortunately, it seems, such partnerships are few and far between. Now back to reality.

Consider now the generally accepted signals.

The Permitted Signals
The signals will usually come into play on your first throw away when you are void of the led suit and you are not able or do not need to ruff to take the trick. You throw away a card which will indicate a message to your partner and there are four popular discard systems of which you should be aware. You and your partner will decide what system you will play and in a club situation your system will be marked on your convention card. I hasten to add – you don't have

to have a discard system. It is entirely up to you and your partner, but it is very useful to be able to indicate to your partner that you have an interesting card. Beware though – none of the systems are foolproof.

But be wary, your signals may be detected by the opposition and they have the right to ask your partner for a description of any discard system should you not follow a led suit and the reply must be truthful.

Revolving Discards. – I like this system the best. Keeping 5's, 6's & 7's as neutral cards, a higher card asks for the suit above and a lower card asks for the suit below. So for example the 9 of Diamonds will ask for a Heart to be led, the 3 of Spades will also ask for a Heart and the 3 of Clubs will ask for a Spade and so on. Hearts are led and you are void and wish for a Spade then you would play either a Diamond above 7 or a Club below 5.

If a suit has been spent, for example, if the trumps have been drawn, then your high card in a suit just below the trump suit will obviously not ask for a trump but the suit above the trump suit. Suppose trumps are Hearts and you are obviously void then a low Spade will ask for a Diamond or a high Diamond will ask for a Spade. The same applies if you are obviously void in another suit. The obvious void suit is skipped when giving your signal.

Dodds – Stands for <u>D</u>iscouraging <u>Odds</u>. If you lay an even card – you want that suit. If you lay an odd card – you want that colour but the other suit. So putting into practice using the 5's, 6's & 7's as neutral cards, the 3 of Clubs will ask for a Spade (odd – same colour other suit) and the 4 of Hearts will ask for a Heart (even card – same suit).

McKenney – The suit I'm discarding is not wanted. After throwing away on one suit and playing a card from a not wanted suit, two suits remain, one of which you would like led. A high card in the *I do not want suit* means *I want the higher of the other two suits*. A low card in the *I do not want suit* means *I want the lower of the other two suits*.

Texas – The suit I want is the suit above the suit I am now throwing away. A Club will mean I want a Diamond, a Spade thrown means I want a Club and a Heart thrown means I want a Spade and that's it.

The Suit Preference Return Signal - When partner is going to ruff the card you lead you can tell your partner which suit to return by the value of the card you play. A high card asks for the higher of the other two suits, a low card, the lower. If you have no preference then a middle order card lets partner make the decision.

Some words of warning. Always bearing in mind that your partner may not be able to give you a signal because the cards for such a signal are not held. In addition a neutral card may not be held either so your partner may have no alternative than to play a card which, if taken as a signal, could mean something completely different.

What you should not do when signalling.

- Draw your signal card slowly and deliberately from your hand whilst eyeballing your partner until you've got your partner's full attention.
- Place the signal card on the table and keeping a finger on the card until you believe your partner has spotted the signal.
- Don't suddenly have to clear your throat when playing a signal card.
- Play the signal card to a different position than your normal play so as to bring that card to your partner's notice.

If you are guilty of any of the above wrongs when signalling then you might as well give up all the underhand body language and movements and just tell your partner what suit you would like led. I'm being facetious of course. I'm saying this because rest assured all your exaggerated movements in trying to pass the message would certainly have been detected by the opposition in any event so why all the subterfuge.

149

Petering – On the first lead you play the higher of a doubleton (not Ax unless partner has bid the suit or Kx) and on the second play of that suit your partner will see a lower card being played from your hand which will tell your partner that you are then void of that suit and can ruff if the suit is led again. This system tends not to be popular nowadays because it gives too much information to the opposition.

However, Petering works better the other way round. If your partner leads an Ace and you have two cards in the suit, apart from the King and one other, play the higher of the two cards first. When your partner leads that suit again you will play the lower and your partner will then know that you do not have any more of that suit and a ruff is on the cards, so to speak, when next that suit is led. If partner plays another master in the led suit you can then **signal** your partner by the card you then throw away, other than ruffing, of course, for the suit you would like led.

Giving information to your partner
You bid in the auction in an endeavour to give your partner some idea of the shape of and points in your hand and also you take notice of the bids by the opposition because those bids will give an indication of their holding. It's no secret. All the bidding is above board and the players have the opportunity of gleaning, over the short auction period, what information is made available from the bidding.

Many players will already have some knowledge about your hand through your body movements and level of intensity when you first look at and sort your cards. That one card which you've placed at one end of your fan – is that a singleton? The big sigh and the scratch of your face surely indicates a poor looking hand and the several obvious recounts with your lips moving as you count will surely develop into a strong opening bid.

Many Bridge players would certainly not make good poker players. Their generosity in providing free information to the opposition at the outset about their hand often continues after the first card is laid on the table and the accentuated discard signal is just one example. Another example is the slight hesitation when holding a King of the suit led by the RHO when the Ace and Queen are in Dummy. What a give away. Then when the hesitation is pronounced in order to give the impression of holding the King when it is not and that, of course, is most certainly against the rules.

Another big give away is as a result of disinterest and it is usually the fourth player who is the culprit, sometimes playing a card before a card has been played from the Dummy hand.

A card is played and another is played by the second player. Out of the corner of the third player's eye, the fourth player is seen as already having selected a card to play and thus quite often the third player wins the trick with a cheap finesse. But then hoisted by ones own petard. The third player has spotted the fourth player holding a card in readiness for play and has chosen a lower card to play with expectation of winning the trick and then be so frustrated when the fourth player puts back the card previously drawn in readiness and then plays another card which wins the trick with a card that would not normally have won the trick.

Metabolic Age.
I watched an interesting programme on Channel 4 last evening about a group of nine ladies and gentlemen whose BMI was greatly in excess of the 25 threshold figure which divides folk into those who should be losing weight and those who need to watch they do not get into a situation where they need to loose weight. My Body Mass Index at the moment is 25.4 so I'm on the borderline but I put the slight excess down to inaccurate bathroom scales.

Anyway what I'm leading up to is the question of my metabolic age because that subject was covered in last night's programme. Those nine people in the programme were ordinary people you see in the supermarket yet their combined metabolic age was well over 100 years more than the total of their ages and that started me thinking.

I was born in the winter of 1940. It's now the Summer of 2008, although it doesn't feel like it, so that makes me 68. Goodness knows what my Metabolic age is according to the Metabolistitians. I know there's no such word, but you know what I mean. In my opinion my MA as I shall call it surely depends upon what I am doing at the time the assessment is made.

When I'm playing badminton on a Friday morning with a group of ladies , yes I'm the only bloke, who, apart from one are in receipt of a state pension, I reckon my MA is 55 during the first two games rising to 65 in the third and 75 during the final game. When removing myself from a car the MA reading will most certainly be 85 and those that actually view my emergence will certainly believe that reading.

The reading would be near 30 when I'm considering playing football with my Grand-Son Jad but the reading rapidly increases to 40 during the first few seconds of play and then shoots up beyond 75 after just one minute when I have to sit down to catch my breath and the same thing applies to another activity, albeit rare nowadays, but we wont go into that. All jokes aside I imagine if I presented myself to one that knows about such things I would be given a metabolic age of about 60 or perhaps I'm kidding myself. Why is the pronunciation of metabolic so different from metabolism?

Let's get on with Fourth Suit Forcing.

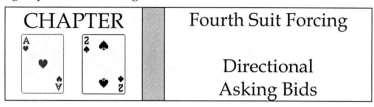

CHAPTER

Fourth Suit Forcing

Directional Asking Bids

Look up the subject of Fourth Suit Forcing in most Bridge textbooks and you will, very likely be provided with a complex explanation. During the many years I have been playing Bridge at local Bridge Clubs I have found the very simple explanation of Fourth Suit Forcing is what players at my relatively lowly level have accepted and the explanation is as follows:

As the heading suggests, it's all to do with the Fourth Suit - the unbid suit. What a surprise. Between you and your partner, three suits have been bid and a fit has not been found so the chances of a game in any of those three suits are pretty small. How about a no-trump contract then?

After three suits have been bid by the partnership, it is a bid of the fourth suit usually on the second or third round of bidding in an unopposed auction that implies the question:

'Partner, as we seem not to agree on any suit, I am interested in a no-trump contract. Do you, by any chance, have a stop in this suit? If so, kindly bid no-trumps. If you do not have a suitable stop in this suit then I leave the final decision to you and good luck. By the way, you should alert my bid because it is not a natural bid and I do not want to be left in the suit I have just bid.'

However, before you ask this question by the bid of the fourth suit you and your partner must come to an agreement as to the quality of cards in the held fourth suit. In bidding the fourth suit one does assume that the bidder does not have proper stop cards in the suit to warrant a no-trump contract hence the enquiry of partner.

Many partnerships demand that at least half a stop is held before bidding the fourth suit enquiry such as – Jxx, Qxx, 10xxx, and Kx and with a guard in hand the player being asked can bid in no-trumps as confirmation. Other partnerships have no such stipulation as to having half a stop in which case the player being asked must have a good stop or two in the bid suit to proceed with no-trumps. Without a stop, the player to whom the Fourth Suit Forcing bid is addressed must bid a suit and the denomination will of course depend upon the earlier bidding.

It is always a bit of let down when you have bid the fourth suit and your partner denies having a suitable stop. Having probably reached the three level in your bidding you then have to try and find the best solution and it is often not very easy because a fit in another suit has not been found.

The opposition are taking note of your difficulties with great interest because at that stage there is a gaping hole in your armour and the opposition will be after a kill.

Talk about helping the opposition.

> Your partner's denial of a suitable stop is good news for the person who is on lead. Weakness has been displayed and unless the partner of the person on lead has bid during the auction then no prizes for guessing what suit is going to be led.

> With this in mind, should your partner deny having a suitable stop in the fourth suit, be very careful about proceeding with your thoughts on a no-trump contract.

Directional Asking Bid

Commonly abbreviated as DAB. It is a low level bid of the opponent's suit which simply invites partner to bid no-trump. The bid asks the question:

"Partner, do you have a stop in the bid suit and if so please bid no-trumps."

The bid will usually occur immediately after an opening bid by the opposition or after an opposition opening bid and two passes. The conventional bid will be used because good cover is held in all suits bar the bid suit.

A very disruptive bid because it takes up one level of bidding. For example, suppose the opposition have opened 1s and you bid 2s asking partner for a stop in Spades. The opener's partner must now bid at the 3 level to respond to partner. By the same token, the player who bids the DAB 2s, in the example, must be prepared for a bad answer because if the partner does not have a stop in the suit then an alternative bid, to a no-trump bid will be made and that will be the best suit at the 3 level in the example, which could well be a 'bid to far'.

The opposition have opened in a suit and you have a strong hand but cannot bid 1nt to show that strong hand because of the lack of cover in the opener's suit. You could double to show an opening hand and shortage in opponent's suit but with a strong hand why not upset the opposition by bidding their opening suit as a DAB enquiry. You will not expect your partner to have much of a hand but hope for a stop when partner will bid in no-trumps.

Do not use the DAB in the fourth position after your partner has overcalled because that could be construed as confirming cover in the opponent's bid suit and asking for partner to confirm strength of the overcall when your partner would rebid overcall suit with points in the lower end of the overcall points scale or bid another suit with points above.

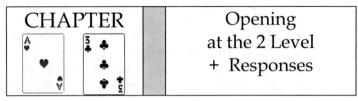

| CHAPTER | Opening at the 2 Level + Responses |

Let's get the easy one out of the way first.

Opening 2nt – You will have 20, 21 or 22 high card points and ideally a stop in each suit and at least two cards in each suit although you might get away with having a singleton Ace. You do not have to by quite so disciplined as to balance as you do with opening 1nt .

<u>Your partner has opened 2nt and the RHO has passed.</u>

   When discussing responses to partner's 1nt opening I mentioned two conventions, Stayman and Transfers. These conventions are not only used after partner's 1nt bid but also after the 2nt opening bid.

Stayman is a 2c bid after a 1nt opening by partner, seeking a four card major. The negative is 2d and the positive is 2h or 2s and if both majors are held then 2h is bid. **Stayman** is also a bid of 3c after a 2nt opening by partner seeking a four card major. The negative is 3d and the positive replies are 3h and 3s. Holding both the reply is 3h.

Transfers – Just as you can use the Transfer convention after partner's 1nt you can also use Transfers after partner's 2nt opening bid in a similar way. 3d transfers to 3h and 3h transfers to 3s and after partner's transfer you can bid 3nt or even more with a slam in mind. At least your partner who opened 2nt will know about the 5 card major.

Some partnerships agree Stayman and Transfers over 1nt but not over 2nt. It is entirely up to you and your partner to agree.

Your partner has opened 2nt and you hold 0-3 points then pass.

Best pass with this hand. You may argue that if your partner has 22 points then game could be missed. You must consider the probabilities. It is more likely that your partner has 20/21 points than 22 points. In fact a 2 to 1 chance.

♠	Q54
♥	J63
♦	9864
♣	853

Your partner has opened 2nt and you hold 4-10 points and are balanced then bid 3nt.

"But I only had four points and they looked a bit miserable at that."

If you hold just 4 points like the hand shown you may take the view that if your partner has only 20 points then you are one point short of the 25 points normally needed for 3nt. Your partner has promised 20 or 21 or 22 points. There is a 2 to 1 chance that your partner will have 21 or 22 points rather than just 20 points and on that basis you should take a chance holding only 4 points and bid 3nt.

♠	J85
♥	Q64
♦	8654
♣	J92

If you have a four card major consider Stayman 3c and if a negative reply bid 3nt. If you have a five card major and more than 3 points then bid the major at the 3 level and partner with 3 card support will bid to game in that major or bid 3nt. If you have a five card major and you have agreed Transfers then bid the suit below your major and your partner will bid the major. You can bid to game or more at your discretion having transferred the play into your partner's strong hand and your weaker hand goes on the table as the Dummy.

It always appears that when Ruth, my Bridge partner of many years is happy with my Dummy hand, when it goes on the table, she says thank you Bryan but otherwise she just says thank you partner. Sometimes when I have misunderstood a situation then I get a short, but very friendly, lesson on what I should have bid.

Consider the bids by holders of these hands after partner's 2nt opening. Note - a response bid of a suit at the 3 level forces to game.

♠	K843
♥	J5
♦	Q43
♣	9863

Try Stayman 3c and if the reply is 3d or 3h then bid 3nt but if the reply is 3s then bid to game 4s.

♠	Q7
♥	984
♦	K97543
♣	43

The long minor may well be very useful to partner in a 3nt contract.

♠	94
♥	KJ954
♦	J63
♣	983

You have 5 points, enough for game. Respond 3h (confirming 5 cards). Your partner, holding 2 Hearts will bid 3nt or with 3 Hearts will bid to game – 4h. If you have agreed Transfers then bid 3d and your partner will know you have five Heart cards.

In opening 2nt, your partner is most likely to have at least two cards in each suit and 20/22 points. You know straight away about the game points and the fit in Spades so bid 4s. If Transfers have been agreed then bid 3h. Your partner will then bid 3s and you will bid to game – 4s and your partner will play the contract.

♠	AJ9743
♥	95
♦	J8
♣	853

♠	85
♥	953
♦	KQ953
♣	852

Best not respond 3d because your partner may think you have more points than you have and may get grand ideas about a slam. Best you raise to 3nt holding this hand.

If you have a hand with more than 10 points then you must consider enquiries about Aces and Kings with a slam contract in mind. It is a shame when holding more than 10 points and you have bid 3nt and your partner has 22 points and a slam is made.

When I have a hand with 22 points, rather than opening 2nt, I seriously consider 'borrowing' a point and opening the conventional 2c which indicates a very strong hand, to be discussed shortly.

Opening at the 2 level in a suit except 2c (as I said a 2c opening bid will be discussed later**).** Opening 2d, 2h or 2s promises at least five cards in the suit and a hand just short of a force to game. Ideally you should be able to see 8 playing tricks but if not the hand will contain 20, 21 or 22 points. If you can see 8 playing tricks then your hand need not have 20-22 points. Sometimes a 17 or so point hand will suffice. As a guide, the five card suit should not be weaker than AQ973 or a six card suit not weaker than KJ10954.

It's relatively easy counting points in your hand but not so easy counting playing tricks. Watch as some folk count the points they have in their hand. Many will 'mouth' the number of points so those players good at lip reading certainly benefit from their skill. Some folk run an index finger across their fan jabbing at the honour cards.

<u>**Counting playing tricks**</u>:
AQJ94 – With this five card suit you must consider the possibility of the King and the ten sitting on your left hand side so you might lose not only the Queen to the King but also the 9 to the 10. However if not vulnerable, I might count these five cards as 4 playing tricks with fingers and toes crossed.

AQJ942 – With this 6 card suit you would likely loose a trick to the King but win the remainder so 5 playing tricks.

KJ10864 – Murphy's law is often very evident in Bridge and you bet the Ace and Queen will be sitting smugly with your left hand opposition. On this hand I would count only 4 playing tricks.

QJ9754 – Taking into account all I've said about the previous holdings, if the wind turns strongly in your favour you may achieve 4 playing tricks but frankly if vulnerable I would not assume any more than 3 playing tricks.

Responding when partner opens at the 2 level (not 2c) in a suit.
With less than 4/5 points bid the negative 2nt but consider my comment in the next paragraph. With 6 or more HCP's give a positive response. If you are able to bid positively, then with mediocre 3 card support for partner's major, bid at the three level but with better raise to game. Without support bid your own suit (if two suits then bid in ascending order) and a bid of 3nt shows a balanced hand and no respectable support for partner's suit. You can jump to your own solid suit holding AKQJxx or AKQxxxx or better

In *The Road Across the Bridge* I said that an opening bid of 2 in a suit was forcing for one round which meant that you must bid after your partner's opening bid and with a Yarborough or less than 4/5 points you bid the negative 2nt. Discuss this aspect with your partner because some players prefer to have a situation where a suit bid at the 2 level is forcing for one round and other players agree that the 2 level opening is not forcing when you pass holding a very weak hand. The problem arises, if you do not have a forcing for one round arrangement, is if the opener has two suits and partner's pass with cards in the unmentioned second suit means a fit and possibly game in the other suit is not found.

As part of your partnership system of play, discuss and agree whether or not the 2nt opening is forcing for one round and if not forcing then the minimum points to be held for a response.

I prefer to have a 2 level opening which is forcing for 1 round allowing the opener to show a second suit and this example will confirm the reason.

♠	AK10987
♥	KQJ94
♦	void
♣	KQ

After a 2s opening, the right hand would not pass but bid the negative 2nt. The left hand then bids 3h and the right hand bids to game – 4h , after adding distribution points to hand for the void in Spades.

♠	void
♥	8632
♦	9642
♣	J8654

My responses to partner's 2 level opening (not 2c) assuming no opposition bids, on the following example hands are as under:

♠	K875
♥	82
♦	953
♣	9643

Partner opens 2s – respond 3s.
Partner opens 2h – respond 2nt.
Partner opens 2d – respond 2nt.

♠	Q5
♥	963
♦	K853
♣	Q963

Partner opens 2s – respond 3nt.
Partner opens 2h – respond 3h.
Partner opens 2d – Respond 3d.

♠	K875
♥	82
♦	Q97
♣	J874

Partner opens 2s – respond 4s.
Partner opens 2h – respond 3nt.
Partner opens 2d – Respond 2s.

♠	974
♥	AKQxxx
♦	void
♣	9752

Partner opens 2s – Respond 3h.
Partner opens 2d – Respond 3h.

On the following hand, if your partner opens 2d then if you have agreed to always say something so that partner has the opportunity of bidding again then bid 2nt otherwise pass.

♠	98652
♥	J752
♦	7
♣	742

Partner opens 2s – Respond 3s.
Partner opens 2h – Respond 3h

The Conventional 2c Opening – The Opener can achieve game or near game with little or no help from partner. Opener will hold one of the following:

23 or more points
(some partnerships open 2c with only 22 points)
or
A hand with three or less losers
as in the 19 point hand illustrated.

♠	AK6
♥	AQ4
♦	KQJ9753
♣	void

**If your partner has opened the conventional 2c
<u>You must bid even with a Yarborough</u>.**

Your partner has opened 2c so you know there is a powerful hand opposite and that the bid in Clubs is conventional. Your partner has a very strong hand and whatever you have in your hand, <u>you have got to bid something.</u> But what?

You must bid and you have two choices and either choice is what your partnership has agreed.

<u>Choice 1</u> is the popular negative bid of 2d which tells partner that you have 7 points or less as simple as that. If you have a 7 point hand and the 7 points are made up by an Ace and a King then <u>do not bid the negative 2d</u>.

<u>Choice 2</u>. Is simply a relay bid of 2d which says nothing to partner about the strength. The opener will rebid in a suit or in no-trumps and the responder will then bid according to the strength of hand.

In the remainder of this chapter I am going to use the popular 2d response as a negative response holding 7 or less points and if exactly 7 points, those points do not comprise an Ace and a King.

If your partner opens 2c then game is most likely and therefore the bidding should not normally stop until a game contract is reached, hence the need for responder to make a bid other than a pass. I say normally because there is the inevitable exception when the responder gives a **double negative** when holding no more than 1 point when the bidding is for example as follows:

First Negative - Opener bids 2c and responder says 2d which tells partner that 0-7 points are held. Opener rebids say 2s.

Second Negative – Responder bids 2nt telling partner that the hand is either a Yarborough or holds only 1 point. It is then up to the opener to pass or bid to game with the sure knowledge of your point situation.

Another Second Negative is a pass after partner has rebid 2nt.

If after your partner has opened 2c and you have responded 2d and your partner then rebids 2nt you pass with no more than 1 point but with 2 or more points then bid 3nt.

2c opening – 2d negative response – 3nt rebid by opener.
Opener has made the decision for game and responder should pass.

Having picked up a strong hand you will be focused on those honour cards that at first add to 21 and then 25 on a second count and then finally at 23 or 24 on the third count. You will not be aware of what is happening elsewhere and with the adrenaline running you excitedly bid 2c and everybody else says wow or words to that effect. Not at a serious club I hasten to add.

Your LHO opposition will normally pass unless he or she has kamikaze tendencies or a very very understanding partner. I say normally because there are genuine reasons why the LHO will bid knowing there is a 'Rock Crusher' hand on the right hand side and those reasons could relate to a hand with say 10 or more points and a long suit. A bid by the opposition in those circumstances does upset the normal flow of bidding by the opener and partner.

But on this occasion the LHO passes and the opener waits with much apprehension for partner to bid. Partner's left hand goes into the bidding box or partner's lips separate and out comes the bid. What a let down and what a disappointment. - 2d. Might as well have not had 23 points in the first place.

As great is the regret when a 2d response is received is the elation when a positive bid is received and that is what I will discuss now.

You open 2c and your partner's bid is anything bar the 2d negative so your partner must have a positive hand of more than 7 points and if only 7 points there is an Ace and a King. Your partner will bid 3nt with 8 or 9 points and no interest in a suit or will bid a major suit at the 2 level or a minor suit at the 3 level. Holding more than 9 points the responder, knowing there is a very strong hand opposite will want to investigate a slam bid, which will be discussed in another chapter, but will wait until partner rebids.

That's all I've got to say on the two level opening so with a few inches of space left on this page I will tell you about my little problem down below. No – it's down further than that – much further. It's almost a ground level problem. I've not consulted the doctor but I do know for a fact that I'm suffering from Plantar Fasciitis which is inflammation of the plantar fascia, the strong band of tissue that stretches from the heel to the middle bones of the foot.

I got to hear about it because Margaret mentioned my problem to a lady at her keep fit class and the lady immediately said *"oh, he's got policeman's heel"* and then my reference to the internet produced Plantar Fasciitis which exactly explained the symptoms.

I had not heard of the complaint before but when I mentioned the problem to me friends they all said "oh yes, Plantar Fasciitis" as if the complaint was as common as a headache. I do feel I should get out a bit more.

| CHAPTER | Doubling |
| For |
| Penalties |

Words of warning about Doubling for penalties. Be very careful when you are thinking about Doubling for penalties because not only do you advertise the whereabouts of the strength which is often better withheld, the Double does give the opposition the chance to take evasive action.

For example; you have Doubled the 4h bid by your LHO and that player, having started off the Heart trail, will be the Declarer. You have Doubled because you hold KJ84 in the Heart suit and a couple of winners in other suits. Having Doubled don't you think the Declarer will have a pretty good idea where the missing honour cards are sitting which will make the decision as to a finesse that much easier. This is what I mean by advertising your hand by the Double.

In addition you also run the risk of the Double failing which will give the Declarer disproportionately high bonus points. Look at the chart showing the figures for a 3h bid being Doubled and the Declarer succeeding in just achieving the contract, achieving an extra trick and an extra two tricks.

Tricks Made	Score undoubled	Score when Doubled & not vul.	Score when Doubled & Vulnerable
9	140	530	730
10	170	630	930
11	200	730	1130

Achieving 10 tricks on a 3h contract will give you a score of 170 which is 30 for each trick over the book of 6 tricks and a part score bonus of 50. If not vulnerable and your 3h contract is Doubled and you achieve 10 tricks then the score is 630 but if you are vulnerable the score is a whacking 930.

But look what happens when the Double is successful. Look at this next chart. Say the same 3h contract is doubled and declarer fails by two tricks by only getting 7 tricks. Not vulnerable the damage is 300 but being vulnerable and failing by two tricks the opposition receive a score of 500. Look what happens when the contract is defeated by three or four tricks.

Tricks Lost	Not Vul	When Vul
-1	100	200
-2	300	500
-3	500	800
-4	800	1100
-5	1100	1400

Doubling for Penalties over 1nt

The opposition, who play a weak no-trump, have bid 1nt and you Double holding 15/18 points with the hope of defeating the contract. Everybody now knows where 12-14 points and 15-18 points are sitting so that does not leave many points in the hands of the other two players who at best have between them 13 points.

If your partner's 1nt bid has been doubled and you have 7 or less points then consider rescuing your partner. You will have already discussed with your partner what the rescue arrangements are in the event of a 1nt bid being Doubled and you will probably agree one of the following by bidding:

a). your longest suit

or

b). a redouble asking your partner to provide the rescue

or

c). 2c also asking partner to bid a suit.

If your partner has Doubled a 1nt opening bid and your RHO has bid any of the above as a rescue, very likely because of lack of sufficient points then you will have some points in your hand and knowing there are between 15-18 points opposite you could consider a game for your side. You only need 9/10 points for a game. If on the other hand your RHO has passed, obviously not worried about the Double then you aught to do something yourself having very few points. Bid your best suit.

Very often the rescue bid is called a 'wriggle'.

166

The Wriggle – is a bid in an attempt to find another contract after a threatening bid by the opposition often a Double. The most popular wriggle is when partner's 1nt is Doubled and a bid of say 2c (the wriggle) is made to give the 1nt opener the opportunity of finding an escape. Another wriggle bid is a Re-Double following a Double of a 1nt opening.

The Bridge wriggle bid came to mind when I was thinking about the vacuum cleaner extension wriggle. Margaret has just posed the second of two questions which I found somewhat difficult to answer. The second question was *'What would you do if I left everything all round the house?'* Some background will help.

This morning I've been clearing up rubbish from parts of the garden and visiting the local household waste department with garden debris and cardboard boxes which I had had in the shed for some time which I thought might come in handy one day. Also taken to the 'dump' were a couple of television sets which again I had stored for some time should they come in handy one day or even back into fashion. After stowing away the trailer I came indoors to shower and get ready for Bridge this afternoon and was politely advised by the cleaning section that she had Hoovered through and would I not drop any bits on the floor. In similar polite tones I advised Margaret that she had in fact Dysoned and not Hoovered which brought a response which I cannot disclose in these pages.

In preparation for my shower I stripped off and of course bits of garden debris fell out of my shirt onto the bedroom carpet and being more than a reasonable husband I collected the Dyson which was standing just outside the bedroom door with the cable hanging in a haphazard way. I plugged in and on my hands and knees with the extension, suctioned up the garden bits and noticed Margaret standing at the bedroom doorway. Whilst Margaret was wishing she had a camera at the ready, I was being particularly mindful of the extension that had slipped from my hand and was wriggling on the floor for fear of what it might attach itself to bearing in mind my naked state and close proximity to the floor.

Then showered and all cleaned up and ready for the afternoon Bridge I had time to spare to set out another set of hands and with fingers poised over the keys, Margaret raised the first question which was rhetorical but I did answer in the negative. *"Did I leave the Dyson where I had found it?"* The second question came in the same breath.

The Penalty Double of a Suit - You will normally Double for penalties an opposition bid at or above the three level and you do need to be fairly confident that you and your partner will defeat the contract because you will pay a high price for failure.

A sobering thought - If you Double an opponent's contract above the 2d level it will give them <u>game points</u> if you fail.

I believe the experts are right when they say that in general, players do not Double nearly enough. I say to you beware –

The ice may not be as thick as you think.

****

CHAPTER		Pre-emptive Bidding

First of all let me answer the question
What is a pre-emptive bid?

In a nutshell it is a very disruptive bid.
A dog-in-the-manger bid
because you do not expect to make the contract yourself
but
you bid to make life difficult for the opposition.

It is an opening bid or an early overcall in the auction at a high level holding only a few points which removes much of the opposition bidding space. The beauty of the pre-emptive bid is that it forces the opposition to guess and go wrong because of their inability to have a proper conversation with their partner and they often end up not reaching a game contract they may have otherwise reached or they end up in no-trumps when they should be in a suit contract or visa versa.

It is however not all roses for the pre-emptor by a long shot. Opening the bidding or overcalling at a high level holding a weak hand may be very disruptive but the bid has a big minus as well as a big plus. The big minus is that you do not expect to make the contract so why bid and run the risk with a high expectancy of defeat? The answer is the big plus. By bidding at a high level at the outset may cause the opposition problems by taking away some of their bidding space and leaving them having to make guesses because they have been unable to have their 'conversation' at the 1 and 2 levels. It's all a bit of a gamble.

But there is another minus. Your pre-emptive bid may result in the opposition finding a game which they may not have otherwise found and in doing so they will have a good note of where a very weak opposition hand is sitting. They will know the pre-emptor will have between 5-9 points and with a bit if counting when the Dummy hand goes down will know the point range of the pre-emptor's partner.

The most usual pre-emptive bid is opening at the 3 level holding 7 cards in suit or the not so common opening at the 4 level holding 8 cards in suit or exceptionally at the 5 level. A pre-emptive bid is also <u>overcalling</u> and with seven cards, the overcall misses out 2 levels of bidding and holding 8 cards the bid can miss out 3 levels of bidding.

Who said Bridge is a friendly game? Overcalling, Doubling and defeating the opposition whenever possible and the pre-emptive bid is just another way of frustrating the opposition. With some prudence and bearing in mind that the bid is made with the expectation of being defeated you should nevertheless not be kamikaze and should make a pre-emptive bid with a modicum of safety and ideally you will have:

a). At least 7 cards in your suit for a 3 level opening
or 8 cards in your suit for a 4 level opening.
and
b). Between 5 – 9 points in your hand.
and
c). Two of the top 3 cards or three of the top 5 cards.
and
d).
<u>If not vulnerable</u>:
can you see 6 tricks in your 3 level opening
or
7 tricks in your 4 level opening?
and
<u>if vulnerable</u>
can you see 7 tricks in your 3 level opening
or
8 tricks in your 4 level opening?

A pre-emptive opening bid holding a weak hand is at the 3 level so you open stop 3c, 3d, 3h or 3s or at the 4 level holding 8 cards in your suit you open stop 4c, 4d, 4h or 4s and be really disruptive. You can imagine the frustration of the opposition having to overcall at the 4 or 5 level to start their 'conversation'.

The pre-emptive overcall misses out two levels of bidding.

> After 1c opening – overcall - stop 3d, 3h or 3s.
> After 1d opening– overcall – stop 3h, 3s or 4c.
> After 1h opening – overcall – stop 3s, 4c or 4d.
> After 1s opening – overcall – stop 4c, 4d or 4h.

An overcall at the four/five level holding 8 cards, misses out three levels of bidding as described and it can get a bit hairy.

> After 1c opening – overcall – stop 4d, 4h or 4s.
> After 1d opening – overcall – stop 4h or 4s or 5c.
> After 1h opening – overcall – stop 4s, 5c or 5d.
> After 1s opening – overcall – stop 5c, 5d or 5h

You can see that by opening the bidding at a high level, how you can cause the opposition a problem because they have to start their own bidding at a high level if they want to be part of the auction. Whilst you wish to disrupt the opposition bidding, you must be very careful not to shoot yourself in the foot. As I have said you may not expect to make the contract but any failure should not exceed 2 tricks when vulnerable or three tricks when not vulnerable. Known as the Rule of 500 in that if you are Doubled you will not loose more than 500 points. If the opposition are vulnerable and they can make game in a major then your sacrifice of 500 is better for you than them taking 620 for making 10 tricks in a major.

You can be a bit 'cavalier' in your pre-emptive bidding when not vulnerable and can afford to go off one or two tricks even when Doubled but be very cautious when vulnerable and best you abide by the four pre-empt rules which I will repeat.

If vulnerable and you want to open with a pre-emptive bid then:

- Do you have seven cards in your suit for a 3 level bid?
- Do you have eight cards in your suit for a 4/5 level bid?
- Do you have between 5 and 9 points?
- Do you have either two of the top three cards or three of the top five cards?
- Can you see seven playing tricks in your hand for a 3 level opening or overcall or 8 playing tricks for a 4 level opening or overcall?

After your pre-emptive opening bid – do not bid again because your pre-emptive bid would have told partner everything there is to know about your hand. Of course there is the inevitable exception. Your partner will ask you to tell him if you have any Aces or Kings should your partner have a high point hand and be interested in a slam.

Here are some hands which have seven cards in a suit and 5-9 points where the opener or over-caller should or should not make a pre-emptive bid.

♠	QJ87532
♥	10
♦	AJ6
♣	95

This hand does have 5-9 points but you should not make a pre-emptive bid. The suit does not have two of the top three cards or three of the top five. Best you pass especially if you are vulnerable because you certainly cannot see 7 playing tricks in this hand. You could however overcall 1s over 1c, 1d or 1h. Although the hand holds only 8 points, having those six spades and that singleton it would be reasonable to overcall 2s over a two level bid by the opposition

♠	9
♥	KQJ9864
♦	J96
♣	95

Looks the perfect pre-emptive hand. 7 points and two of the top three cards. If not vulnerable you should open - stop 3h but if vulnerable, best you pass because only six tricks can been seen. Although only 7 points you could overcall 1h over bids of 1c or 1d and even overcall 2h over 1s. Distribution is good.

♠	Q8
♥	void
♦	KQJ9854
♣	9753

You would open 3d on this hand whatever the vulnerability because with that doubleton Spade suit and the void in Hearts the likelihood of the opposition having the wherewithal for a game in a major is high so start off and be a nuisance. Impede their bidding. Make them start their enquiries at the 3 level.

If your 7 card suit is a major and you have four cards in the other

♠	AQ97532
♥	QJ74.
♦	3
♣	10

major then do not open at the 3 level because you could be defeated in the long suit and find that your partner had four cards in your other major but was unable to investigate because of your opening pre-emptive bid. Much better to open 1s on this hand and see what develops. Your partner may respond 2h.

As said a pre-emptive opening bid is not restricted to the 3 level. With eight cards you can pre-empt at the 4 level and sometimes at the 5 level. Imagine the problem the opposition then have in trying to establish a suit themselves. Look at the following hands:

♠	AKJ87643
♥	85
♦	Void
♣	J74

Not 7 cards but 8 and very likely eight tricks in Spades.
This hand is surely worth opening 4s.

♠	Void
♥	85
♦	J74
♣	AKJ87643

Same structure as the hand above but this time the 8 card suit is a minor with severe shortages in both majors. If not vulnerable and I mean not vulnerable then open the bidding – stop 5c. Can you imagine the opposition with a strong holding in the majors having to overcall and open their bidding at the 5 level.

Can or would I change my plans for next Thursday evening because Dot has invited us out to dinner and look at the dust on this shelf were words from the lady who is about to leave me for the day to do things with our daughter. Shopping I suspect. I was quite excited about the invitation out to dinner until Margaret answered my enquiry as to whether the inviter would be paying the bill. Then the carpet in my study was put straight followed by the customary kiss and goodbye.

Now where was I. Oh yes, the previous hand opened the bidding with a very impressive - stop 5c leaving the opponents in a quandary as to a bid or a double.

There's me saying that to open pre-emptively at the 3 level you need 7 cards and at the 4 level you need 8 cards but now, as you have come to expect with Bridge, are the inevitable exceptions as shown in the next two hands.

♠	AQJ1094
♥	7
♦	J10965
♣	3

Now look at this hand. 6 cards and a second long suit. I'm suggesting you could open 4s if not vulnerable but 3s if vulnerable. I realise you cannot see 7 tricks but you can make allowances for the two long suits. Don't forget you have a partner opposite with 13 cards.

♠	7
♥	KQJ8643
♦	void
♣	QJ1084

It looks as though there are about 8 tricks. Open 4h with any vulnerability.

Be mindful of the Rule of 500.

If you are not vulnerable and you open with a dodgy pre-emptive bid and the vulnerable opposition Double you as opposed to bidding their major contract, you can afford to be defeated by up to three tricks. 100 penalty points for the first trick and 200 for each of the next two tricks. If the opponents could reach game in a major when vulnerable then they would have gained 620 against gaining just 500 for Doubling and defeating you by three tricks. Care when vulnerable because for the first trick the penalty is 200 and 300 per trick for the next two tricks. Therefore being doubled when you are vulnerable and being defeated by three tricks gives the opposition a whacking 800 points.

We'll now have a look at what you should do if **your partner has opened pre-emptively** and no intervening bid by your RHO

Don't be tempted to bid just because partner has opened and you have more than a few points yourself. Your partner's hand is point/weak and length/strong so you must be point/strong to consider a bid yourself. Don't bid after partner's pre-emptive bid unless you've got a strong hand of say 15 or more points bar the exceptional cases I will explain. Bid to game in a major if holding a strong hand with 15 or more points, and a trump or two.

Bearing in mind that the opposition will do all they can to stop you reaching the long suit in the pre-emptive hand, only bid 3nt after a minor pre-empt having stops in the other suits and 3 entries to the long suit across the table when vulnerable especially if the Ace is missing or if the Ace is in hand then 2 cards including the Ace should be reasonably but not necessarily safe. Obviously 3 would be better. An Ace or a King in an opposition hand will not necessarily fall when the Declarer wants it to fall and hold-up play by the opposition often results in defeat.

I know I'm labouring the point but just consider what you would do if the opposition were in a no-trump contract and you held the West hand in the

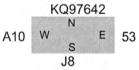

illustration. South is Declarer in a 3nt contract and obviously planning to reach that long suit after the Ace has been played. But the Ace is not played until it has to be played on the second round by which time South is void and unable to reach those cards in Dummy unless there is a winner in another suit which is often unlikely because of the 5-9 point pre-emptive opening.

If you are relying on making tricks in the pre-emptive suit it is unsafe to bid 3nt unless you are confident of being able to reach that suit and therefore you should have three cards in hand and even then a problem will arise if the other three cards, including the Ace are held in one of the opposition hands and Held-Up.

There are occasions when you need to break the rules for common sense to prevail. Suppose your partner has opened 3s and you hold say a 10/11 point hand and a couple of Spades and a void or a singleton Heart for example. After your partner's opening pre-emptive bid, the person on your right hand Doubles, a Take-out Double, asking partner to bid a suit and guess what suit is likely to be bid – Hearts. After the Double you bid 4s and if the player on your left now wants to reply to partner, it will need to be at the 5 level which might make life uncomfortable for the opposition – what a pity.

Here are some replies to partner's pre-emptive bid with no intervening bid by the opposition.

♠	AJ95
♥	85
♦	AK8
♣	J865

Your partner has opened 3h and you have the other suits covered so you must bid 3nt. **You do not.** Suppose for instance your partner does not have the A♥ and the opposition player with that card ducks the first round and maybe the second round holding three cards, which will doubtless happen. How do you then get across to your partner's Hearts after that, having become void of that suit, unless partner has an entry in another suit. Far too many potential losers so best you pass. Of course, your partner may have the Ace and King but suppose the other four Hearts are split 3/1 and the Queen is quietly sitting in the three card holding.

♠	KQ64
♥	Void
♦	AQJ93
♣	J852

Your partner has opened 3h. Surely you must bid something but what? The best bid is pass. If you bid 3nt, how do you propose to get across to partner's Hearts without the help of the opposition and they will certainly not come forward in that direction. You could lose three Clubs, the Ace of Spades and a Diamond plus any Hearts which are not covered across the way.

♠	J
♥	AQ974
♦	KQ75
♣	AQ8

Your partner has opened 3s. Again no entries into partner's Spades so 3nt is out of the question. With all those points and a fit in Spades (partner's 7 + your singleton) then bid 4s.

Now what's best when the opposition are trying to be disruptive and have opened with a pre-emptive bid.

As the pre-emptor is weak, 5 – 9 points, then the chances of the other partnership being strong are good and the pre-emptor's partner should not bid without a strong hand as has been demonstrated. However if the pre-emptive opening bid by the opposition is uncontested at your turn to bid then holding a good hand yourself you should bid. Don't let that pre-emptive bid, intended to upset your bidding plans, succeed.   What do you do holding that reasonable looking hand?

Bid 3nt
With a good opening hand, stops in the suits including a good stop in pre-emptor's suit.

Bid your own suit.
Having 14-17 points and a strong 5/6 card suit.

Bid a minor suit at the 4 level.
Must be strong 17/20 points and only about 5 losers.

Jump to game in a major.
Having 17/20 points, at least six cards and about 5 losers.

The most popular bid after an opposition pre-emptive bid is the **Take-out Double** – *"tell me your best suit partner."* If you would Double a one level opener then you should Double a three level opener – both are for take-out. Your partner will then give you the best suit or pass, having a strong holding in the bid suit or with stops in the bid suit will consider 3nt. After your take-out Double, and partner's bid, other than pass when your partner will be holding good stops in the opening bid suit, you can then decide what to do for the best.

Always ask for an explanation of a Double after partner's pre-emptive opening because it could be the Fishbein Convention which is a defence against a pre-emptive opening and is a Penalty Double. Under the convention a bid of the cheapest suit is for take-out.

Now look at this situation. There has been a pre-emptive opening bid at the 3 level on your left. Your partner has passed as has the opener's partner.

**You are sitting in the fourth position
with 9/10 points and a non-descript hand.**
You would probably pass and so would many bridge players.
After all you've nothing to write home about
and your partner has passed.

Would the situation be any different if you had another 3 or 4 points? If the answer is yes then Double (for take-out) and you will probably find that your partner has more than a few points but was unable to bid and by your Double a fit is found. Look at it this way. The opener will have 5-9 points so assume an average of 7 points. That leaves 33 points in the other three hands. If you have got 10 yourself then that leaves 23 points in the other two hands and therefore the chances of your partner having more than a few points is, don't you agree, quite high.

Be careful though because a). you could push the opposition into a game they would not have found and b). find yourself in a contract which will fail. Just watch the vulnerability.

The Strong Pre-emptive Bid.
Before we finish with the pre-emptive bid, you may pre-empt at the four level with a strong hand of up to 15 points. This is best done when not vulnerable and after partner has passed or after opposition have opened at the 1 level because then the chances of missing a slam are slight. Holding a strong hand do not pre-empt at the three level because if your partner passes as is likely you might miss a game contract. In second place, either pre-empt to game or bid normally at the cheaper level to see whether partner has anything to say.

Still with the disruption of the opposition bidding in mind
we'll now consider a bit of gambling.

A bit of gambling!!!

The Gambling 3nt Opening Bid

You will hold at least seven cards in a minor suit including the AKQ
and holding the AKQ is a must. Partner will pass with stoppers in
the other suits. The theory is that opener will have 7 solid tricks and
partner will have two making the 9 tricks for no-trumps. This pre-
emptive opening prevents the opposition making hay with their long
suit unless they want to overcall at the 4 level. Without stoppers in
the other suits, which in practice is normal, then responder will
simply bid 4c which opener will pass if that is the long suit or bid 4d
if Diamonds is the long minor and that will end the bidding as far as
the pre-emptor is concerned.

Your partner has opened at the three level in a suit
A word of warning.

If you feel your partner has overstepped the mark or has
unwittingly got into a poor situation and you've a weak hand
yourself best not to try a rescue.

However, if the vulnerability is your way and by that I mean the
other side are vulnerable and you are not, then think about it,
because you can be defeated by three tricks Doubled when not
vulnerable and the other side will achieve fewer points than if they
were able to reach their vulnerable contract.

Just A Thought.

If you are sitting in the fourth position after three passes, what is the
point of a pre-emptive bid? At that stage you are certainly not going
to upset, frustrate or make life difficult for the opposition.

To finish this chapter on the pre-emptive bid, this North hand is so distributional that an opening bid of 5c is very reasonable should the vulnerability be with East /West

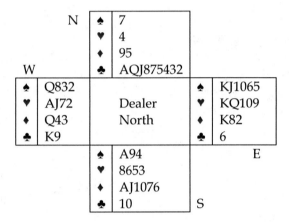

North bids - stop 5c out of the sheer desire to be a dog in the manger. Not confident of being able to get game but will bid in an attempt to stop or hinder the opposition reaching their game in a major.

East is now very frustrated and thwarted; just what North wanted East to be. If East wants to get into the auction, then a Double or a bid of a suit at the 5 level will need to be made. If North is left with the 5c contract then East will lead the K♥ which confirms the holding of the Queen.

If Declarer can get across to the Dummy hand via the Ace of Spades then the return lead of the 10♣ and the finesse of the Queen in hand will secure the King on the next round and whoopee – contract made. Even if the contract fails by one trick when vulnerable and Doubled the reward to the opposition is not nearly so great as their reward for achieving game in a major especially if vulnerable.

Bridge is such a friendly game.

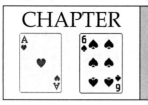

CHAPTER	Slam Bidding
	Gerber & Blackwood
	Cue Bidding
	The Quantitative Bid

You have now reached the stage when you will have an idea of the strength of your partner's hand by the bidding and you certainly know what you have in your hand. Holding 33 points between you and your partner should be enough to make a Small Slam and 37 for a Grand Slam but invariably you and your partner will have distributional hands where suit length is of significance rather than points. With a slam in mind it is very likely no positive signs or sounds have come from the opposition.

When you consider a slam may be on the cards so to speak, you will want to be sure as to the whereabouts of the missing Aces and possibly the missing Kings and to do this you will use one or more of the popular conventions namely:

- Cue Bidding.
- Gerber or Laddering Gerber.
- Blackwood or Roman Key Card Blackwood.

It does seem to me that Cue Bidding has become a forgotten art and it is such a shame when the tool is so handy. It is so useful before embarking upon the very popular Blackwood convention when bidding can get to an uncomfortably high level when an escape to safer ground is difficult if not impossible. Many inexperienced players seem to have an urge to jump to the Blackwood conventional bid 4nt, when an unsatisfactory answer from partner can create such a big problem. It is as if the impulse to jump into Blackwood to locate Aces and Kings is implanted in the inexperienced player at birth so to speak and something that must be done. Much better to seek an Ace or two and perhaps a King by Cue Bidding.

Cue Bidding.

In Cue Bidding, the partners are able to show each other specific Aces, Kings, Voids and Singletons. <u>After a trump suit has been agreed</u> the first time another suit is mentioned will confirm the **Cue Bid** as having first round control holding an Ace or a void and also an interest in a slam. Cue bidding is very useful when you know you have values for a slam but do not know whether you and your partner have full control of a particular suit. For example – Suppose you open 1d and your partner bids 1h, holding the hand shown (delayed game raise), and you, with 15 – 17 points, bid stop 3h.

♠	KJ4
♥	KQ864
♦	K84
♣	A9

At this stage the partnership has agreed
the trump suit as Hearts.
<u>No doubt about that.</u>

The responder holding this hand, knowing about your 15-17 points obviously has interest in a slam. The Heart suit has been agreed as trumps and now the responder, holding that A♣ will bid 4c. It is a <u>Cue Bid</u> and confirms the first round control of Clubs as either an Ace or a void in Clubs. If you, the opener now <u>Cue bids</u> 4d then that confirms the first round control of that suit in either the Ace of Diamonds or a void in Diamonds. If the same suit is bid again by the same player or by the responder as will be the case here, then that will confirm the second round control of Diamonds – the King.

Once you have agreed a trump suit then <u>Cue bid</u> which says to partner: *"I am interested in a slam. Instead of bidding Blackwood now I am telling you that I have control in the suit I am bidding and control means that I have the Ace or I am void of the suit. Please tell me if you have control of any other suit."* After the Cue bid the responder's first responsibility is to tell the Cue Bidder whether or not he/she is interested. If not interested then bid the agreed trump suit at the next level, probably game level. However, if interested then the responder can bid another suit to show a first round control or bid partner's Cue bid suit to show second round control such as the King. If partner has control of two suits then the lower suit should be bid first.

If your partner, by Cue bidding, confirms the first round control in any other suit then you can confirm the second round control of that suit, for example the King, by bidding the suit at the next level.

An example of Cue Bidding.

Opener				Responder
1d	KQ5	♠	AJ4	1h (delayed game raise)
	AQ96	♥	KJ542	
stop 3h	KQ8752	♦	J9	3s (cue bid)
	void	♣	KQ7	
4c (cue bid)				6h.

Opener bids 1d. The responder immediately knows that game is on and is interested in partner's rebid so responds 1h to see what partner says next. At this stage all the opener knows is that there is at least 6 points and four hearts opposite. Holding 16 points (15-17) the opener will jump one level and bid stop 3h to support partner.

The responder now knows for sure that partner, the opener, has 15-17 points, at least five Diamonds and four card support for Hearts. With that knowledge the responder now believes that a slam is worth seeking. Knowing that Hearts will be the trump suit, the responder will now tell partner that the first round control in Spades is held so responder now Cue Bids the Ace of Spades by bidding 3s.

Back to the opener who now knows that partner has points for a slam having Cue bid and knows that partner has either the Ace of Spades or a void in Spades. To continue the conversation the opener will now Cue bid the first round control in Clubs showing either the Ace of Clubs or a void in Clubs. The opener will now bid 4c and with that information the responder will bid stop 6h.

Had the responder used any of the other systems for seeking aces, shortly to be explained, then the result would have been two missing aces and the 6h slam would not have been bid <u>because other systems do not confirm the existence of a void.</u>

Another Cue Bidding Example where <u>Cue Bidding</u> confirms the suit
of an Ace before embarking upon Blackwood.

West				East	
♠	AJ53		♠	K98642	
♥	AJ104	Dealer	♥	82	
♦	Q93	East	♦	A	
♣	84		♣	AKQ2	

East opens 1s and West counts losers and responds stop 3s. There is
only one Heart loser because of the Jack and Ten being together.

Holding that singleton Ace and the good control of Clubs, East
has a Slam in mind but is worried about those two Heart cards. East
is worried, because if the opposition have the Ace and King of Hearts
and Hearts are led then it will be 'curtains'. Instead of bidding the
Blackwood 4nt asking for Aces, East, knowing that Spades will be
the trump suit, will start the cue bid process by bidding 4d
confirming first round control of that suit. First round control means
either an Ace or a void.

West also knows that Spades will be the trump suit and
recognising partner's <u>Cue Bid</u> of the Ace or a void in Diamonds will
show the first round control in Hearts by bidding 4h which is just
what East wanted to hear because now East can proceed to
Blackwood (covered later in this chapter) with confidence that the
Heart suit is controlled.

East bids 4nt, knowing that partner has
the Ace of Hearts and is pleased when
West replies 5h confirming two Aces. East
then bids 5nt asking for Kings and West
replies 6c which means no Kings and East
settles for 6s.

Whilst cue bidding is a
very useful tool, you
obviously cannot use it
if you do not have the
boss cards or voids and
as such you will need to
resort to one of the
other Ace and King
seeking conventions.

The Gerber Convention – In days gone by it was standard practice to use Gerber only after no-trump bids but now I find the convention used generally. I have an arrangement with some of my partners who for some reason do not use the Cue Bidding system, that if 4c is bid then it is to be taken as the conventional Gerber Ace asking bid unless, of course, it is blatantly obvious that 4c was intended as an ordinary bid having already bid Clubs twice for example.

Your partner bids conventional 4c asking for aces
then you reply as follows:

Holding no Aces or 4 Aces you bid 4d
Holding 1 Ace you bid 4h
Holding 2 Aces you bid 4s
Holding 3 Aces you bid 4nt.

Your partner then may wish to know about your
King holding so now bids conventional 5c.

Holding no Kings or 4 Kings you reply 5d
Holding 1 King you reply 5h
Holding 2 Kings you reply 5s
And Holding 3 Kings you reply 5nt.

Your partner and then the opposition, I hasten to add, will then know how many Aces and Kings you have in your hand and your partner will complete the bidding accordingly.

North				South	
♠	K75		♠	AQ6	
♥	K74	Dealer	♥	AQ9532	
♦	K96	North	♦	A	
♣	QJ94		♣	K72	

North opens 1nt and South, holding those 19 points, immediately has designs on a slam, particularly holding those 3 Aces. South bids 4c and North replies 4d, having none and then South bids 5c. North then replies 5nt having 3 Kings. Whilst one Ace is missing, South knows that partner has the K of Hearts and with confidence bids 6h.

A word of warning. The Gerber bid is 4c as I have explained. If you use the Cue Bidding system it is best to use the Gerber convention only after a 1nt opening because the 4c conventional Gerber bid may be confused with a 4c Cue Bid and you could get yourself in to a mess.

Laddering Gerber

Some folk call it progressive Gerber. I find this convention most effective and keeps the bidding at a relatively low level should you receive poor answers to your Ace and King seeking bids.

You agree with your partner that the 4c bid is solely reserved for seeking Aces except for those cases when your 4c bid will be so obviously natural. You have reached the stage in your bidding when you want to ask for Aces and Kings so you just bid 4c (Gerber) and your partner will respond as normal. When you want to find out about the Kings you do not need to bid 5c. All you do is to bid just one step higher than the bid you had from your partner as the answer to your 4c question.

An example of the Gerber Convention (not laddering)

Opening bid	Opens 1nt	Responder	Stop 4c (Gerber)
♠ J4		♠ AQ105	
♥ AQ10	4h (one ace)	♥ J65	5c (for kings)
♦ QJ106		♦ AK8	
♣ Q1095	5d (no kings)	♣ AJ7	5nt

In the above two hands the three kings are missing hence the escape into 5nt. Now see how the use of <u>laddering Gerber</u> with the same two hands, bring the bidding to a conclusion at 4nt and not 5nt.

Opening bid	Opens 1nt	Responder	Stop 4c (Gerber)
♠ J4		♠ AQ105	
♥ AQ10	4h (one ace)	♥ J65	4s (for kings)
♦ QJ106		♦ AK8	
♣ Q1095	4nt (no kings)	♣ AJ7	pass

After opener's 4h bid confirming one ace, the responder then bids 4s (one step up the ladder) asking for Kings.

Another example. You bid 4c and your partner answered 4h showing 1 ace. Instead of bidding 5c for Kings you bid 4s being the next bid up from the 4h answer you had. Your partner will then use your 4s bid as the starting base and reply as follows – 4nt no kings or 4 kings, 5c for 1 King, 5d for 2 Kings and 5h for 3 Kings.

Another example. Your partner bids 4c and you have 2 Aces you will answer 4s. Your partner will then bid 4nt asking for Kings and with 1 King you would answer 5d.

Another example. Your partner has no Aces and replies 4d. You then bid 4h asking for Kings and with no Kings or four Kings the answer would be 4s, with 1 King 4nt, with 2 Kings, 5c and with 3 Kings 5d.

Compare this with Blackwood, which follows, when you have reached uncomfortable levels when finding out that your partner does not have the required equipment for the slam bid. With laddering Gerber you do have an easy escape.

The Blackwood Convention - There should never be any hurry to use this convention because it is always available when you reach the four level, so why not take the sensible route and use the lower levels to continue your exploratory conversation by using a Cue Bidding system and then Blackwood if necessary.

Let's look at the Blackwood Convention. A bid of 4nt and then 5nt is the Blackwood 'Ace & King asking' Convention. It works like this:

The Ace seeking bid is 4nt and you reply as follows:

If you hold no Aces or 4 aces you will reply 5c
If you hold 1 Ace then you should reply 5d
Holding 2 Aces you reply 5h
And holding 3 Aces you would reply 5s.

Then the King seeking bid 5nt and you reply as follows:

Holding no Kings or 4 Kings you would reply 6c
Holding 1 King – 6d
Holding 2 Kings – 6h
And Holding 3 Kings you would bid 6s.

Consider the following North and South hands where the partnership have been unable to cue bid and resorted to Blackwood in an attempt to find the missing Aces and Kings. In this instance, although the trump suit has been agreed early in the bidding process, cue bidding could not be used because South did not have a void or an Ace. In other words, South did not have first round control of any suit other than the agreed Heart trump suit.

North		South	
♠ AJ	Opens 1d	♠ KQ82	Responds 1h
♥ Q1093		♥ AK876	
♦ AQ986	Stop 3h	♦ J	4nt (Blackwood)
♣ K4		♣ QJ10	
	5h (2 aces)		5nt (Blackwood)
	6d (1 king)		6h

South, holding those 16 points immediately knows that game is on for sure but instead of showing the strong hand straight away will bid 1h knowing full well that, having changed the suit, partner will bid again and partner's rebid will be very informative in that it will confirm either a weak or strong opening hand.

North does have a strong hand 15-17 points rather than a very strong hand 18-19 points and jumps in partner's Hearts and bids stop 3h.

South is now interested in a slam, knowing there are about 16 points opposite but will not Cue Bid because the hand does not have an outside Ace or a void so on this occasion the Blackwood convention is the answer. South bids 4nt. North replies 5h confirming 2 Aces and South then bids 5nt asking for Kings. North replies 6d confirming just one King. South, somewhat disappointed, now knows that there is 1 Ace and 1 King missing but nevertheless will bid that slam – 6h.

Consider the following two hands. The partnership do not cue bid but they have agreed ordinary Gerber in priority to Blackwood.

Opening bid		Responder	
♠ KQ	Opens 1c	♠ AJ105	Responds 1s
♥ AK10		♥ J65	
♦ QJ10	Rebid stop 3nt	♦ AK8	4c (Gerber)
♣ A10952	(19 pts reverse)	♣ Q73	
	4s (2 aces)		5c (Gerber)
	5s (2 kings)		6nt

Although 1c was the opening bid, a bid of 4c after the strong opening hand has been revealed is obviously not a natural 4c bid and obviously Gerber. Had the opposition been involved and the bidding had crept up then the 4c bid would have been natural.

A little tip	Another little tip
When you know that Clubs are going to be the trump suit then you need at least two Aces in your hand to bid 4nt because if your partner answers 5d (having only 1 Ace) then you will need to bid 6c which may be too much.	If your partner is engaged in an Ace and King seeking exercise then do not overrule your partner because your partner is in charge. Just answer the questions.

And yet another little tip

If you and your partner have not found a trump
suit then best not use the Cue Bidding system.

If you are not familiar with using Cue Bidding then there is a lot to be said for not using Blackwood at all. The dangers of using Blackwood and not the Cue Bidding procedure.

- Blackwood will tell you how many Aces there are in your partner's hand but it will not confirm the suits unless obviously all the missing aces are confirmed.
- Do not use Blackwood when you have a losing doubleton in a suit that has not been bid. A missing Ace and a missing King could be in the same suit.
- If you are missing two Aces and after Blackwood your partner confirms holding just one Ace then you will not know the suit of your partner's ace.
- Suppose you have agreed Clubs as your trump suit and you are missing three aces and bid Blackwood 4nt. Your partner holding only one of the three missing Aces will respond 5d leaving you to bid 5nt or 6c with two missing Aces.

Use Blackwood by all means because it is a good tool for finding out about the number of Aces and Kings but use the Cue Bidding system as well because whilst you may have specific information about the suit of one particular ace, the Blackwood convention will tell you about any other Aces and Kings.

Compare Gerber or better still, in my opinion, Laddering Gerber with the Blackwood convention when you have reached uncomfortable levels when finding out that your partner does not have the required equipment for the slam bid. With Gerber you do have an easier escape.

A popular variation to the Blackwood Ace/King seeking bidding system is **Roman Key Card Blackwood.** There are the four aces and the King of the agreed trump suit which are all considered to be key cards. So this variation of the Blackwood convention will seek 5 key cards and the King of the agreed trump suit is considered to be the fifth ace or the fifth Key Card. Obviously it is very important for a trump suit to have been established before initiating Roman Key Card Blackwood.

If the partnership have agreed to Roman Key Card Blackwood then the ordinary Blackwood 4nt conventional bid is used and the replies are as follows:

5♣ shows 0 or 3 Key Cards
5♦ shows 1 or 4 Key Cards
5♥ shows 2 or 5 Key Cards without the Queen of Trumps
5♠ shows 2 or 5 Key Cards with the Queen of Trumps

The Quantitative Bid – 4nt

The 4nt bid usually asks for Aces but when bid straight after 1nt or 2nt opening bids, it is not Blackwood but an immediate invitation to 6nt. A bid of 4nt like this by responder after partner has opened 1nt or 2nt means that responder has enough points for 6nt provided opener has top of the point range the bid confirmed.

Put it this way, if you held 19 points and fairly balanced and your partner had bid 1nt then you know that the partnership has at least 31 points – partner's minimum 12 and your 19. If your partner had top of the 1nt opening range of 14 points then you would have 33 points between you and enough to bid 6nt. Or if your partner had 22 points and opened 2nt and you had 11 points then again you would have 33 points and enough to bid 6nt. Bear in mind though that having 33 points is no guarantee of making the slam because the missing 7 points could be an Ace and a King of the same suit.

> Allegedly said by Dummy to partner who had bid and played a Grand-Slam which had been Doubled. *"How unfortunate you failed by one trick on your Grand-Slam bid. How on earth were you to know that the Ace of Trumps was in one of the opposition hands?"*

The quantitative bid of stop 4nt asks partner the question – *"if you have the top of the range you have already confirmed by your opening 1nt or 2nt bid then bid 6nt"*. Your partner either bids 6nt or passes having recounted the number of points in hand.

191

North			South	
♠	QJ107		♠	AK83
♥	K92	Dealer	♥	Q87
♦	K96	North	♦	QJ3
♣	QJ10		♣	AK7

North opens 1nt. South, holding a balanced 19 points hopes partner has 14 points in hand because if so a slam is possible. South bids stop 4nt – a **Quantitative bid** which says to partner – *"I have enough points for a slam if you have top of your range. "* In this case North has only 12 points and will pass. With 14 points North would have bid stop 6nt and with only 13 points North would have cogitated – good or bad 13 points.

Again if your partner had opened 2nt, you would know there were 20-22 points opposite and with shape and enough points in your hand to contemplate 6nt then ask the same question by bidding 4nt. *"Please partner if you have the top of the range you have already confirmed by your 2nt bid then bid 6nt"*. In either case with 13 points or 21 points, the opener would consider whether the points were good or bad and bid accordingly.

North			South	
♠	AKJ		♠	Q52
♥	AJ7	Dealer	♥	Q98
♦	K874	North	♦	AQ53
♣	AQ2		♣	J53

North opens stop 2nt holding 20-22 points and balanced. South has 11 points and with maximum points opposite a slam is on the cards. South bids stop 4nt which is a **Quantitative bid** asking partner to bid to 6nt holding maximum points in the range already confirmed or pass if holding the minimum. North does in fact have 22 points the maximum so is happy to bid 6nt. Holding 20 points North would have passed and holding 21 points would have tossed a coin – good or bad 21 points.

Whilst on the subject of Little Slams and Grand Slams, I thought it apt to mention the Declarer's euphoria when successful. Quite right too because the Declarer deserves to be overjoyed and self satisfied but not to excess and this is where the word hubris would appear to describe the arrogance or excessive pride exhibited by some experienced players. You know, sitting back, chest out and a wide beam across the face.

My command of the English language is not that good in spite of my advanced years but having said that I could say that my command of Bridge play technique is not that good either.

At the Bridge club some while ago a gentleman at the table mentioned the word hubris which he repeated after my '*I beg your pardon*' and repeated again after my reference to being unfamiliar with the word. He gave an explanation in a very scholarly fashion which later that evening nearly matched the definition in my dictionary but did explain his partner's look of self satisfaction or shall I say smugness having just taken 13 tricks.

Having had the word highlighted so to speak, I've seen the word printed in the newspapers on several occasions recently. I suppose it is similar to the situation when you have agreed to buy a new car, for example and then every time you go out you see the same model time and time again; that model not being that conspicuous before.

- *A certain gentleman was plea-bargaining with prosecutors and his resignation speech was a creepy mix of hubris and denial.*

- *He had lost control of the company's finances and a string of profit warnings followed. Hubris, lack of preparation and arrogance were suggested.*

- *The television programme The Apprentice is about watching beautiful egomaniacs squabble, exhibit delicious hubris and get eventually skewered by the boss.*

Fortunately hubris is not evident very often at the Bridge table but self satisfaction or quiet smugness by the Declarer will occur at any one of four points when a slam has been bid.

- The look of satisfaction that will lighten the face of the Declarer when seeing straight away that the slam is certain when partner's Dummy hand goes on to the table.

- When latterly during the play a vital card is played by the opposition. The squeezing and pouching of the Declarer's lips and the involuntary nod of the head tells all.

- When a vital finesse is successful. The same body language as if Declarer had received a letter from the Inland Revenue promising an unexpected refund of overpaid tax. The expression on the face of the Declarer shows an intensity of emotional excitement. A large intake of air and a relaxation of muscles.

- When, on the penultimate round, a vital card is played which makes Declarer's last card a winner giving the Declarer the contract. Self satisfaction is very much in evidence and sometimes perhaps a little unintentional hubris may be evident. That success and feeling of well being will continue through to the next round.

The Defenders do have to take care though when the Declarer is breezing though the card play at a rate of knots. So confident with the outcome the Declarer could well face half a dozen or so cards and claim the remaining tricks in such a confident manner that a potential winner for the Defenders may be missed. The Declarer faces the cards and says words like *'I'm going to ruff the 3 in Dummy, cross back to my Spades and then back to Dummy with the 7 of Diamonds..................'.* So overcome with the Declarer's confidence and manner, the Defenders are often seen to accept the situation without question.

On the other hand self satisfaction or smugness by the Defenders will occur at any one of two points when a slam has been bid by the opposition.

- When it can be seen, following the Dummy hand being tabled, that the contract is doomed.

- When, later in the play, the Defender knows a card in hand will most definitely defeat the contract especially if that card is as a result of clever card play.

Then the thoughts of a glum Declarer who's little or grand slam contract is doomed from the start after the Dummy hand goes on the table.

- Idiot partner. Incorrect Blackwood bid.
- Why on earth did you jump in spades?
- Why did you jump holding only 14 points?
- Are you never going to learn?
- You knew my 4c bid was a Cue bid and not Gerber.
- I want to go home.

So yes – hubris – arrogance and having a superior manner towards those considered inferior. I hope I do not unconsciously exhibit delicious Hubris.

I've just had a thought though. Perhaps I do exhibit hubris on occasions. What occasions? Those occasions when Margaret has for example jumped in her support for my opening bid or enquired through a fourth suit forcing bid and I find that her bid, when her hand goes on the table as Dummy, was justified.

Hubris and yet more Hubris
All those years of Bridge tuition have not been in vain.

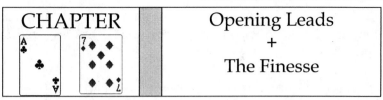

CHAPTER | Opening Leads
+
The Finesse

What card to lead at the outset is often a bit problematical and sometimes downright difficult? The choice of lead is made a little easier if your partner has bid during the auction. The choice of a card to lead is not made any easier by the fact that so many contracts fail and succeed only through the opening lead and thus it is important to think carefully before you draw that first card from your fan. You will have many occasions when it is not practical to lead a card from three suits and are left with only one suit from which to lead the first card and you are not that relaxed about that either.

When I'm sitting left of the Declarer and thinking what the dickens to lead I consider:

- Did partner bid?
- What did the opposition bid?
- What card would the Declarer like me to lead?
- What suit would the Declarer like me to lead?
- What card/suit is least likely to benefit opposition?

On the third and fourth above just consider for a second the card and suit the Declarer would like led. Imagine yourself looking at the Declarer and asking the question. 'Mrs Declarer, please tell me what suit and what card would like me to lead' and then looking at your fan of 13 cards, imagine the answer.

'Would you like me to lead my unsupported Ace of Hearts?'
'Yes please, because I've the King which will then definitely make.'

'I've this unsupported King of Clubs. Would you like that led?'
'Ooo please, what an angel. My Ace will take the King and then my Queen will make a trick. Thank you very much you are a sport.'

I won't go on with this silly imaginary conversation but you will by now have got the message. You are not there to assist the opposition in any way.

Now some do's and don'ts on the question of leads and I'll start with leading against a no–trump contract.

Opening leads against a no-trump contract:

<u>Firstly the do's in the following order of importance</u>
- Lead the top of an <u>internal</u> high sequence such as the Queen from AQJ97. If the King does not appear then **do not lead that suit again yourself but wait until partner leads the suit back to you through Declarer.** If partner holds the King then that should be played to unblock. Also lead the J from KJ1086

- If you are not able to lead the top of an <u>internal</u> high sequence then lead the top of a high sequence. Lead the King from KQJ86 or the Queen from QJ1097. **If the high card or cards do not appear then keep on leading until they do.**

- If your partner has bid during the auction then lead off the top card in partner's suit. The Declarer will have stops in your partner's suit having bid after your partner called but sometimes the stops are a bit wishy-washy.

- If you do not have a high internal sequence or a high sequence then lead the fourth highest form your longest suit.

- Unless partner has bid the suit do not lead a suit where you hold either the Ace or the King. If you have to choose from two long suits like K953 or 8542 lead the lowest of the second set because you are more likely to make the King in the first set.

- Leading an unbid suit is often a good choice because that suit is often the opposition's weakest suit. Always consider leading the unbid suit even with a shortage of cards.

I do have a problem with Margaret about the fourth highest. In my book from K9864 the fourth highest is the 6 but Margaret then tells me that the 6 is the fourth lowest. No, I say, it is the fourth highest. The King is the highest, then the 9, then the 8 and then the 6. Margaret still thinks it is the fourth lowest so you do see what I am up against.

And now the don'ts when leading against a no-trump contract.

- Do not lead from a short suit unless partner bid that suit.
- Do not lead a suit bid by the Declarer.
- Do not lead Aces or unprotected honours.

Now some thoughts on the opening lead against a suit contract.

A lovely lead is a singleton in any event especially of suit bid by your partner because if your partner has the Ace, a possibility, then an early ruff can be achieved. Do not lead a singleton King because if holding the Ace and the Queen, the Declarer may try a finesse and loose the Queen to your singleton King and then be thoroughly frustrated when you subsequently ruff the Ace, provided of course, you have not been stripped of trumps by that time. If you are able to ruff the Ace, just have a glance at the exasperated expression on the Declarer's face.

If you have a suit headed by an AK then lead the Ace which will allow you to see what cards are in the Dummy hand for free so to speak whilst still retaining control.

Unless partner has bid the suit, do not lead away from an Ace or a King. For example holding this hand when Hearts are trumps, do not lead the K♠ or away from the King say the 3♠. Do not lead the A♦ or away from the Ace say the 4♦. Holding this hand the best card to lead is the 3♣ which will indicate to your partner that you hold an honour. How?

♠	K873
♥	8
♦	A954
♣	Q853

As you do not lead away from an Ace or a King then the card you lead will indicate whether or not you hold a Queen or a Jack. Lead a low card like the 3 from Q973 and that will show a Queen or Jack but lead a high non-honour like the 8 from 98742 and that will confirm no interest in that suit.

See how the lead works in practice on the following two illustrated hands.

Take the 3♣ lead from the West hand and look at how the Clubs are spread in the four hands. Once the Dummy hand goes on the table, East will know that partner is holding the Queen. If Declarer asks North to play the King, which is doubtful, East's Ace will win the trick but if any other card is played from Dummy, say the 9, then East's Jack will win the trick.

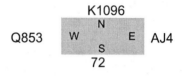

The lead of the 8, a high non-honour card, from the West hand will indicate no interest in that suit and East will know that an honour in partner's hand is unlikely.

Most folk would not lead away from an Ace against a suit contract for one simple reason. Where is the King most likely to be if the suit has not been bid by your partner? You've guessed it. I always work on the premise - <u>Aces kill Kings</u>.

A recap on leading against a suit contract.?

- Lead a singleton in the hope of a ruff on the second round.
- Lead an Ace if holding AK.
- Lead a King holding the Queen.
- Do not lead away from an Ace or a King.
- Lead a low non-honour to show a Queen or Jack
- Lead a high non-honour to confirm honour not held.
- Discretionally lead a high card in suit your partner has bid.

If you lead a King, Queen or Jack then it will be from a touching honour so the card immediately below will be held. That's what your partner will understand.

Try and lead a suit not bid by the opposition but if you have to lead a bid suit then choose the suit bid by the Dummy hand.

If partner has overcalled a suit during the auction then at least five cards will be held and the suit should be of decent quality so much so that the over-caller will not mind if that suit is led.

Do not lead from a doubleton in a suit bid by the opposition. By all means lead the top card in a non-honour doubleton in an <u>unbid suit</u> (called Petering) and if partner has the Ace and leads the suit again your playing the lower card will indicate a void on the next round and ready for a ruff.

In conclusion then.

Avoid these opening leads.

- Never under-lead an Ace unless of course, it is your wish that the Declarer makes a trick with the King. In other words, if you hold A963, best not lead this suit.
- Never lead an Ace unless you hold the King as well.
- Do not lead a singleton trump. It may destroy your partner's trump holding like Jxxx or Qxx or even Kx.
- Never ever lead a singleton King.
- Do not lead away from a King in a suit contract. Always consider the likelihood of the Declarer having the AQ. That King in your hand behind the Declarer will be a nuisance.

If your partner has doubled the suit contract for penalties and you hold an honour trump then lead that card because otherwise your partner will correctly believe the card is sitting in Declarer's hand and the lead of the honour could well promote trump cards in your partner's hand.

If you have a three card suit without an honour then lead the middle card, then when next the suit is lead play the higher and then the lower. It's call MUD – Middle, Up, Down and then you are ready for a ruff. But having said that, by the fourth round so is almost everybody else.

Now thoroughly confused I expect you will do what many players do and that is to pull a face, sigh deeply, stare at partner for inspiration and then pick a card from the 13 in hand having appeared to have completely ignored the auction.

When I am the Declarer I am not only interested in the card that is led but also very interested in the facial expression of the player on my right hand side, because often there is something to be read. You'll get that very smug satisfied look when the right card and suit is led and also that *'why the dickens have you led that card'* look when the wrong card is led. The latter is the same look I give a certain lady in my life when the opposition have ruffed and she could have taken the trick with an over-ruff but was not following the play sufficiently enough to notice what had happened.

Some folk regularly lead a singleton trump when defending a suit game contract. I do not understand why because if the opposition were to ask me, as Declarer, what suit I would like them to lead, I would invariably say *'a trump please.'* especially when I'm sitting with the AQ. Leading a singleton trump could damage your partner's holding of Jxxx or Qxx or Kx because otherwise your partner would stand a reasonable chance of making the J, the Q or the K.

When I am Declarer I often welcome the opening lead of a trump but having said that, there are occasions when I want to benefit from a shortage of a suit in Dummy in order to win extra tricks by ruffing and the unreasonable action by the opposition in leading trumps at the outset has spoilt my plans.

The opponents have dominated the bidding and your partner has done nothing but pass throughout the auction.

The bidding went 1h -stop 3h – 4h
What is your opening lead holding this hand?
♠963   ♥86   ♦KQ105   ♣AJ74

Best lead the K♦ confirming the Queen. Do not lead the Ace of Clubs because of the likelihood of setting up tricks for the Declarer. If the Declarer is holding the King, that Ace could be a killer.

What about the following bidding where your partner took some interest and overcalled Spades as in this auction. Your LHO opens 1d, your partner overcalls 1s, your RHO bids 2h and your LHO wins the contract by bidding 4h.

What is your opening lead holding this hand
♠K8   ♥85   ♦KQ105   ♣97432

As your partner has bid Spades then lead the King of Spades which you hope will hold in the expectation that your partner holds the Ace. After a second round of Spades you then hope for a ruff. After the high-low with the first the King and then the 8 your partner will know you only had two Spades. You Petered.

Before discussing the Finesse just let me remind you something when you are considering the card to lead. Just ask the Declarer what card or what suit is required as an opening lead. Of course don't literally ask but just imagine and consider what answer you would get and see how often it works.

One more. You are to defending a 3nt contract and you are on lead and your partner, other than passing, said nothing during the auction.

What is your opening lead holding this hand

♠AQJ95 ♥85 ♦K965 ♣92

Partner has not bid so no clues there. You have an interesting Spade suit with an internal high sequence – QJ9. Lead the Queen and if it holds then do not lead that suit again but wait for partner to lead the suit to you through the Declarer when capital will be made.

Now The Finesse -

The Simple Finesse 1.

South is the Declarer in a suit contract. Declarer leads a low card and West also plays low. South does not know

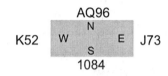

the whereabouts of the King. South has to decide on whether to play the Ace and definitely win the trick or finesse the Queen, hoping that the King is sitting in the West position and not played. Declarer decides to finesse the Queen which wins the trick.

The Simple Finesse 2. -

Declarer at South plays the 10 and West plays low. Declarer decides to finesse the 10 which wins the trick. The finesse has succeeded. The lead is still with South who now leads the Queen which draws West's King which is beaten by the Ace.

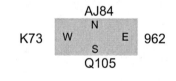

Swap the East/West hands around.

South plays the 10 and finesses but the missing King is played from West to win the trick. A failed finesse attempt.

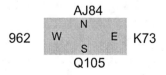

Where is the missing honour card?

When considering the finesse, take into account the bidding during the auction because if a suit has been bid by one of the opposition players then the likelihood of honour cards of that suit being in the hand of that opposition player is greater than them being with the other opposition player. A finesse is therefore worthwhile; never certain of course. If South does not finesse and plays the Ace in the above hands, the King, provided it is not a singleton, will definitely make a trick on the next round of that suit. If South's finesse is unsuccessful then what has South lost because had South played the Ace, the King would have made a trick on the next round of that suit.

So by the finesse you do give yourself a sporting chance and you make capital if the finesses come off.

Then the times when missing the King, you lead towards AQJ and finesse the Queen which wins the trick. At this stage you believe the King is sitting in the hand of your LHO. Back into your hand you lead another with the expectation of being successful with the Jack or take the missing King with the Ace and then find the King sitting behind Dummy which takes the trick. Very frustrating and not very sporting, but after all, it's all fair play. If you are the one who held up the King on the first round, just look at the expression on the face of the player who was expecting to make the trick thinking the King was in your partner's hand especially if your play defeats the contract because Declarer could not reach winners in Dummy.

The Deep Finesse 3.

During the auction the opposition have made a bid but have lost the contract which is now with N/S playing in no-trumps. North is Declarer and is very aware that West

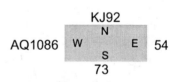

made a bid during the auction but having adequate cover in the suit was not perturbed. Declarer will play a low card from the South hand and West also plays low. Taking account of the bidding during the auction North now plays the 9, which is a deep finesse, which wins the trick. In playing low, West had hoped North would have played one the high honours. That's the deep finesse.

Three weeks ago, the lady I was scheduled to play with last night, had better things to do with her time it seemed and I was left stranded without a partner but luckily a charming gentleman who had been called Norman for a considerable number of years was also without a partner for the same reason and last night we sat opposite each other for the first time. During the five minutes we had together before the game, we quickly discussed tactics and decided on Stayman and Transfers over 1 and 2 no-trumps, Dodds signalling and Gerber in preference to Blackwood unless it was obvious Clubs was to be the bid suit.

Everything went fine until I opened 1nt and my partner bid 2c. I announced Stayman and bid my only four card suit which was Hearts. My partner then bid 4c and assuming it was the Gerber Ace asking bid, I replied 4h holding just one Ace and then my partner bid 6s with which I was completely satisfied on the basis that my partner would know what he was doing or so I thought.

We went four tricks down and it transpired that my partner's usual arrangement with his regular partner is that if Hearts are mentioned after a Stayman enquiry then it is showing Spades. The moral of the story is clear. When you meet a new partner for Bridge, do not leave yourselves just a few minutes before the game to discuss tactics.

CHAPTER

Notes on
Card Play

I'm going to finish with some notes on card play. By now I know you will not run away with the idea that I am anywhere near being an expert at Bridge card play. Far from it and for that reason I will not spend too much time on the subject other than to give you a few broad notes. You will develop your own style of play and learn from your mistakes as I have and I am still learning from mistakes, sometimes very silly mistakes.

The opposition, often in a most pleasant manner, will do all they can to defeat the contract just like any game and by the same token the Declarer will endeavour to make as many tricks as possible. With this in mind both the Declarer and the defending players should always consider the following for starters:

What would the opposition like me to do?

What suit would the opposition like me to lead?

What card would the opposition like me to play?

Would the opposition like me to play this card now?

Would the opposition like me to ruff?

Never ever do what the opposition want you to do.

Situation 1. The contract you hope to make is say 3nt and the opposition have led a 6. The Dummy hand goes on the table which shows the 973 in the led suit and you have the AK4 in hand.

What would the opposition like me to do?

Simple answer. The opposition would very much like you to win the trick with the Ace and then lead the King.

Do not do what the opposition would like you to do.

What you should do is the opposite. Duck the first round and play the 4. The suit will be led again straight away so play the King. When later the suit is led again as it inevitably will at the first opportunity, you will play the Ace by which time your RHO will very likely be void of the suit and then later unable to lead back that suit to any remaining winners in the hand of your LHO.

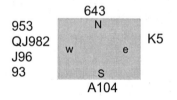

West correctly leads the Q. East rightly overtakes and plays the King and South wins the trick with the Ace. <u>What a bad move by South</u>. East is going to hold on that very important 5 because when next on lead that card will be played to West's winners and as you can see West would not be able to lead again, having no winners in other suits. South should have ducked the first two rounds and then win the trick with the Ace on the third round.

The other important aspect here is the decision by East to play the King over partner's Queen. Remember that Queen could have been either the top of an internal high run or the top of a high sequence and therefore important cards were held in hand with the intention of defeating the contract hence the lead of the Queen. East plays the King to unblock

Do not return the opposition led suit unless, of course, it is to your advantage.

Situation 2 - South has unwisely bid 3nt following North's 3s pre-emptive opening bid, having good stops in three suits but only two cards in partner's suit. Obviously South wants to set up partner's spades as soon as possible and will lead a spade at the first opportunity.

West now thinks
What does Declarer want me to do?
Answer - Declarer obviously wants me to play the Ace and win the trick.

KQ98643
98
J53
10

A5

N
W E
S

J2

107

West will not do what South wants and will duck the first round and play the 5. Having only two cards in the suit the Ace will win the next round but by then South will have no cards in the suit to get across to those remaining 6 winners and there are no other winners in North's hand.

When your partner has shown particular length in a suit such as a pre-emptive bid, you must be mindful of the times you are able to cross the table bearing in mind that the opposition will not assist. You would normally be reasonably safe with three cards and could perhaps take a risk holding the Ace and another but with anything less you should be very cautious.

Situation 3 – You are sitting South as Declarer and the 7, for example, is the first card played. You must play low from Dummy because whatever happens, you will achieve one trick. If East does not take the trick with either the King or Ace, Declarer will win

J85

N
7 W E
S

Q62

with the Queen. If East does take the trick, the Jack or the Queen will later become a master. If you play the Jack on the first round you will likely loose both the Jack and the Queen.

Situation 4 – do not take all the trumps from opposition hands until you have dealt with something to your great advantage.

You are Declarer at South in a Spade contract and West has led a Heart at the outset. North's hand goes on the table as Dummy. Take the trick but **do not** then go about relieving East and West of their trumps before you have dealt with a situation that has arisen which will be to your advantage.

♠	752
♥	J
♦	KQ43
♣	76432

N

Dealer

S

♠	AK963
♥	A753
♦	97
♣	AK

Win the Heart trick with the Ace in hand and then lead another Heart and ruff in Dummy. Then get back to your hand via a Club and lead another Heart and again ruff in Dummy. Then try to get back into your hand again via the last Club to repeat the process. If the Hearts are split evenly then you will have made three tricks with Dummy's miserable trumps without spending any in hand. Very economical.

Situation 5 – Try to foil Declarer's attempt to make cheap tricks. If you see the situation looming where Declarer is attempting to make cheap tricks by ruffing in Dummy then do what the Declarer does not want you to do and that is to lead trumps and foil the little plan by taking trumps out of the Dummy hand. Even if you only manage to achieve one round of trumps, you may have saved one trick. Be careful though, do not take steps to thwart the Declarer and shoot yourself in the foot.

Situation 6 – I've touched on this situation already. The opposition are in a no-trump contract and your partner's opening lead is the K♣

♠	965
♥	7542
♦	J874
♣	A3

You hold this hand. You must overtake and play the A♣ otherwise you will block your partner. If you do not play the Ace, you will win the next round of Clubs and then be unable to lead that suit to your partner's winners. Remember, the King lead is from the top of a sequence so your partner will have the Queen and probably the Jack as well. Your best action is to overtake partner's King with your Ace (**to unblock**) and then lead back the 3♣.

209

Situation 7 – If the Ace is seen on the table in Dummy and Declarer leads the Queen, you should play the King. It just means that the opposition have spent two high honours against your one.

Situation 8 – Think carefully about the cards in your hand and the cards that have just appeared after the first lead by your LHO. Look at these two hands with the Declarer at South playing a 3nt contract. West leads a low Diamond.

	N	Dummy
	♠	732
	♥	KQJ85
	♦	KQ
	♣	1096

What Declarer must NOT do is to play a low Diamond card from hand because if the 3♦ is played then how will Declarer get into the Dummy hand to cash Heart winners if one of the opposition have Axx and **duck** the first two rounds when Declarer will become void – and helpless.

	S	Declarer
	♠	AK105
	♥	762
	♦	A3
	♣	KQ54

What Declarer must do is to think about the situation when the first card is led and then sensibly decide to overtake the Dummy card in hand with the Ace and then lead Hearts straight away. If the Ace does not fall then Declarer will play the boss Hearts until the Ace does appear and then using the low Diamond to get back into the Dummy hand for the remaining Heart winners.

Situation 9 – The opposition have bid to a Slam in no-trumps and you are on lead. You will know that they have enough points to have bid their no-trumps slam. If you have a long suit headed by the Queen or the Jack and say five or six points in hand then I consider it wise not to lead that suit and the reason is this. If you have a few points yourself then your partner is likely to be very short on points and your lead from a long suit headed by a Queen or a Jack could be just what the opposition want. Your Queen or Jack could win a trick if that suit is lead towards you.

Hesitation – If you ponder over whether to play a particular card and then play another card, inevitably the Declarer will know you have something to hide and will take full advantage of your hesitation. The most common 'give away' is when the Declarer is attempting a finesse. For example, the Ace and Queen are in Dummy and Declarer leads a low card from hand. You have the King and you hesitate and play a low card. The Declarer spots your hesitation straight away and therefore the chances of your having the missing King are high and Declarer plays the Queen and wins the finesse.

What you must never ever do is to hesitate with the intention of making Declarer believe you hold the missing card when that card is not held. In the same way, if you hold a singleton and that suit is led then you must not hesitate on purpose to give the impression that more than one card is held so as to take advantage from a subsequent ruff when that suit is led again.

Always play fairly and do not try to gain an advantage by body language, or exaggerated hand movements when playing a card. What's that famous quotation by Confucius – What you do not want done to yourself, do not do to others.

Are there any stray Red Indians in the hills? – It's childish I know but consider the trumps in opposition hands as Red Indians in the hills. If you do not draw all the trumps then you run the risk of not having a safe passage through the valley with another suit. If you and the Dummy hand have a lengthy suit then it stands to reason that the chances of a ruff by the opposition are high. Why risk playing an Ace and having it ruffed when it will make a trick after the Indians are out the hills. I am certainly not saying that you should always draw all the trumps out from the opposition but just be mindful that trump cards in the hills will take tricks.

There is a well known saying in Bridge circles. 'There is many a man walking the Embankment, sleeping on the streets of London, who failed to draw trumps.' Then there is an extension to that well known saying '........sleeping on the streets of London and an equal number pulled out at Westminster Bridge who drew trumps too soon.'

Without thinking I have sometimes drawn trumps from the opposition hands only to realise that I have stripped myself of trumps and been unable to ruff a short suit. It is usually best to draw opposition trumps but not to your detriment and remember, if the opposition only have one trump left and it is the master trump, why spend two of your trumps to draw that card which is going to win a trick in any event. It's called the Rule of One.

Is your ruff at a high enough level? The greater the number of times a suit has circled the table the greater is the chance of a ruff cropping up. Be careful, when considering a ruff because that cheeky LHO may take the liberty of playing a higher trump to win the trick.

Always cash your winners in the short hand first. This is most important when you do not have an outside entry to the hand with the length and the remaining winners. Look at these situations:

J7	facing	AKQ84	Play the Jack first
K8	facing	AQJ4	Play the King first
A82	Facing	KQJ73	Play the Ace first
Q82	Facing	AKJ7	Play the Queen first.

Certainly not sharp practice. I quite like fooling the opposition into believing a situation exists when it does not and the following will emphasis the point. I am Declarer and the Ace of Diamonds is led. There are three rubbishy Diamonds in the Dummy hand and I have the Queen and a rag – meaning a non honour. Knowing full well the Queen is going to be taken in any event by the King on the next lead of Diamonds I play the Queen on the Ace thus giving the impression that I am then void of Diamonds and ready to ruff the King. Nothing wrong with that. It is so good when the action causes the opposition to resist leading that suit again straight away and I love the expression on the face of the opposition player when I subsequently throw away a small Diamond. Sharp practice!! Good play.

In the last week or two Margaret has been going through a new for old spending spree and I'm concerned that the current mood for replacing the old will include me. I often feel these days, especially after 9 o'clock each evening, that I've got about as much second hand value as the furniture which is about to leave the house. By replacing me, at least Margaret, who is still in very good condition for her age, stands a reasonable chance of getting a chap with a full head of hair and a thicker tread on his trainers.

We needed a new dining room table and six chairs. The word needed is not quite correct because we already have a dining table and six chairs in almost immaculate condition which would have seen me out and probably the kids as well. Put it this way, if you are of the female gender in this establishment then a new dining table and six spanking new chairs are definitely needed plus a new sideboard and another cabinet. Total cost – a few pounds short of a sizable sum. When the new furniture arrives, the old but very well maintained and almost scratch free table, sideboard and cabinet, which have been part of our married life for donkey's years, will be loaded onto my trailer and taken to a charity shop or down to the dump. Is it still alright to call the local recycling centre – the dump? Why did we need the new furniture? – Don't ask me, something to do with fashion. The chairs? They will be put into the loft and brought out when visitor numbers exceed the number of new chairs just ordered, which I hope will not be that often.

The reason I'm telling you this is because I've just taken up badminton again after a break of some 10/15 years, with the intention of prolonging life. Last evening the foot-ware worn was, as far as I am concerned, not only extremely comfortable but very suitable for prancing around on the badminton court with a lot of other oldies, but not suitable, according to her ladyship, for a man in my position, whatever that means. This morning I succumbed and £24.99 later brand new trainers are ready and waiting for me to wear tomorrow. In fact they are on my feet at the moment being broken in, just like me when I was first married. What will happen to the old pair? I'll probably put them in the drawer of the old sideboard at present intended for the dump.

Still wondering when I will need replacing.

The discussion about the new badminton footwear costing £24.99 has not come to an end and it is the cost that is the crux of the matter as to why the topic is still the subject for debate.

As you know by now I am Mr Average and very uncool and thus probably boring. The only time I am cool is when the temperature drops and I am not wearing the proper clothing. Taking today's parlance from those who have not yet experienced life beyond 20 years, I take the view that it is very cool to be uncool. The footwear I purchased for badminton is coloured white and very comfortable but unfortunately the name on the side of each item is not the name one should have on the side of each item if one was cool. It does seem that to be cool, I would have had to spend over £70 on the footwear.

I get all this vital information from my daughter Mandy who for some reason probably to do with the temperature, prefers to spell her name Mandi. Her partner Jason, who is positively very cool, according to Mandy, would not be seen dead in the footwear I purchased. I will definitely have the last laugh though. My £24.99 trainers will see me out whereas Jason's cool footwear costing mega bucks in comparison will need to be changed next year for fear of being seen as out of fashion.

My tee-shirts are also extremely uncool in as much as they do not have motifs printed on the front and back, understandable by only those aged 25 years and under. I must admit the style of an item of my clothing which is not normally seen by the general public, not even the waist band, is ice cold but very comfortable. At least I do not walk round the street demonstrating textile reorganisation which can quite often put one out of step.

Before getting on to other popular conventions outlined in the next chapter, I thought tables of expected points under various circumstances would be useful as a guide so here goes.

The points promised by the opener.
No opposition intervention

Opening bid 1nt – weak no-trump		12-14
Opening bid in a suit. 10/11 points = 6 cards or 2 x 5 card suits 10/11 points also could mean the rule of 20		10 - 19
Opening bid in a suit at the 1 level and after partner's 1 level suit response, the opener	Rebids 1nt Rebids 2nt Rebids 3nt	15-16 17-18 19
Opening suit bid at the 1 level and after partner's 2 level response in another suit opener rebids	Rebids 2nt Rebids 3nt	15-16 17-19
Opener's bid in a suit and without partner's support then rebids that same suit at the 3 level		15-19
Opener bids in a suit at 1 level and can then support partner's major. But in a minor a no-trump bid is sought before game in a minor.	Next level Jumps 1 Bids Game	10-14 15-17 18/19
Opener bids in a suit and then rebids in a lower sequence suit		10-14
Opener bids in a suit and then rebids in a higher sequence suit		15 or more
Opening bid 2nt		20-22
Opening at 2 level in a suit With less than 20 points = 8 playing tricks.		20 -22 or less
Opening bid at the 3 level	7 cards	5-9
Opening bid at the 4 level	8 cards	5-14

The points and cards the opener would expect partner to hold with no intervention by the opposition.

Responder bidding 1nt.		6 – 10
Responder bidding a different suit at the 1 level. (May be a delaying game bid)	4 cards at least	At least 6
Supporting opener at the 2 level. (Min. 5 points with partnership agreement)	4 cards at least	6 –10
Bidding 2nt after a 1 level suit opening		11/12
Bidding 3nt after a 1 level suit opening.		13 (+)
Bidding at 2 level in different suit. Some partnerships insist on at least 9 points.	5 cards	8 (+)
Jumping in major opening. Some partnerships expect higher number of points	Losing trick count	8+
Jumping in a different suit.	5 cards	15-18
Bidding 3 level in major after 1nt.	5 cards	11-18
Bidding 3 level in minor after 1nt.	5 cards	11 +
Bidding major at 4 level after 1nt.	6 cards	10 (+)
Bidding 2d after opener's 2c		0-7
Bidding 2h, 2s,3c or 3d after 2c opening		8 (+)
Bidding 2nt after a 2 level opening		0-3
Bidding another suit after 2 level opening		6 (+)
Passing after 2nt opening		0-3
Bidding 3nt after 2nt opening.		4/10

Other indications of points & cards held.

Partner doubles opposition 1nt		15-18
Partner bids 1nt after opposition suit bid	Cover in suit	15-18
Partner overcalls at 1 level. Some partnerships demand at least 9 points	5 cards	8-15
Partner overcalls at 2 level	5 cards	10-15
Partner overcalls at 3 level	5 cards	12-15
Partner doubles after two opposition suits.	Other 2 suits	10+
Partner's Sputnik Double	4 cards	6-10
Supporting partner's overcall		5+
Partner doubles opposition 1 level bid	Shortage	10+

The AGM at my local Club, unlike most annual meetings, will be a very pleasant evening. Arriving at about 6.30, I will join with a pre-arranged party of three at a table, which will be dressed with a white cloth and furnished with four sets of cutlery, side plates, a pot of flowers, napkins and most importantly four wine glasses. A committee member will be seen with a bottle of red wine in one hand and white wine in the other filling glasses as they become empty or nearly empty. Within about half an hour the AGM will be finished and a Ploughman's meal is set out for all to help themselves.

After the meal, prepared by the lady committee members, what I call 'funny Bridge' will ensue. Players sitting North will stay put, those sitting South will move up one table, East will move up two tables and West will move up three tables and after four games the same happens again. For an hour or so players will be well mixed. No time to discuss methods of play because it just doesn't matter

I said 'funny Bridge' because the Director for the evening will suddenly announce that after a set of cards have been dealt the contract will be such and such and will announce the compass position of the player who is to play the contract which may be 5d by South, 4s by North, 4h by West and 3nt by East. Also after a deal and after normal bidding, the Director may ask players to take four cards from hand and pass them to the player on the left hand side.

The last hand of the evening is the pièce de résistance or the piece of resistance as one elderly lady called it. After the deal the North/South players stay in place and the East/West players will be asked to leave the table with their cards. During the short absence from their opponents the pairs are to combine their hands and produce one very good hand and then return to the table and bid in the normal way. As you can imagine the likelihood of a slam is high.

Each person has kept a personal score card and the player with the highest score will win a bottle of spirits and the player with the lowest score a bottle of wine and just after 10.15 we will all go home having had a most enjoyable evening.

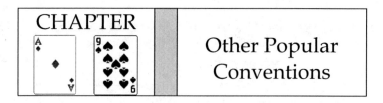

CHAPTER — Other Popular Conventions

In the latter part of my first book, *The Road Across the Bridge*, I mentioned very briefly some of the popular conventions used at my local Bridge clubs. I gave a brief commentary on several but only just a few lines on others because the book was intended for newcomers to Bridge and I did not want to cause any unnecessary stress. They would have been stressed enough already.

The conventions I mentioned were

Transfers
Unusual No-Trump
Modified Pottage
Sharples
Landy
Michaels Cue Bid
Benji Acol
Multi 2 Diamonds

And I also mentioned opening the bidding under the Rule of 20.

In this book I have covered in detail the very popular bids commonly known as Transfers because I considered the convention an important part of bidding. The other conventions I've mentioned are popular but you will be able to have a decent game with friends and at your local Bridge club without detailed knowledge.

I know of many very experienced players whose names are always at or near the top of the club result sheets yet they use only Stayman, Transfers, Gerber and Blackwood. I will now describe all these conventions apart from the Multi Two Diamond bid which I will leave for another time.

Starting with the Unusual No-Trump and Michaels Cue bid. Both are conventions that lets your partner know that you are 'two suited' following a suit bid at the 1 level by the opposition.

The Unusual No-Trump

It is a jump bid of 2nt after a 1 level suit opening by opposition, usually showing the minors and not necessarily having near or opening points. It is the pre-emptive nature that makes the hand biddable having length in both minors and at least 5/5 shape. Both suits should have not less than two honours. After a 1h or 1s bid by the opposition you would bid – stop 2nt and that would be the unusual no-trump.

If your high card point strength is outside the two long suits as in this hand then best not bid 2nt after a 1h or 1s bid by the opposition. Best pass because you are far too weak.

♠	A9
♥	K
♦	Q8542
♣	J7642

An interfering bid in as much as your LHO will need to bid at the 3 level to stay in the bidding. Your partner must bid should your LHO pass and your partner will either bid the best of the minors held, at the 3 level or higher or with good stops elsewhere perhaps consider 3nt.

Some partnerships today use the convention to show the majors when the opposition open in a minor.

Pass a stop 2nt at your peril. Occasionally I have been guilty of not concentrating on my partner's - stop 2nt bid and on each occasion I've receiving the deserved look from across the table.

Your partner has suddenly bid 2nt after your LHO has opened 1s and your RHO has passed. The first message is very clear – YOU MUST NOT PASS. Always bid one of your partner's suits and never be tempted to bid your own suit because you will end up out in the street with no visible means of support. Unless of course you have tremendous strength in your suit when it would be stupid to bid anything else.

Michaels Cue Bid – is the direct cue bid of the opponent's suit to show 5 or more card length in two other suits with at least one of the other suits being <u>a major</u>.

Over minor suit opening a Michaels Cue bid will show both majors. After say 1c or 1d opening bid by the opposition you would bid 2c or 2d which would show partner 5/5 or better in both majors.

Over a major suit opening a Michaels Cue bid will show the other major and an unspecified minor.

As in the Unusual No-Trump the Michaels Cue bids are usually pre-emptive in nature and playing strength and suit quality is more important than high card points. When bidding either of these two conventions, because of the pre-emptive nature you do not need to have many points and quite often only 7+ will suffice.

Many players will wish to bid normally holding intermediate strength of say 10-15 points and saving the Michaels Cue bid for hands with only 5-9 points.

As well as using the Unusual No-Trump bid in the second position after your RHO has bid you can use it just as well in the fourth position after your LHO has opened, your partner has passed and your RHO has responded. For example – after 1h by your LHO, your partner's pass and a bid of 2h by your RHO, you can bid 2nt which shows both minors. Similarly by using the Michaels Cue bid, 1h on your left hand side, pass by your partner and 2h on your right then 3h by you is a Michaels Cue bid showing Spades and an unspecified minor.

Be very careful and use your judgement - When using either the Unusual No-Trump or the Michaels Cue bid you are providing information not only to your partner but to the opposition who will obtain quite a clear picture and if you do not buy the contract your bidding these conventions may work against you. The message therefore is clear. Only use these bids when your hand meets all the requirements for playing strength and suit length.

It does look as though I am trying to talk you out of using these two conventions when I add another warning. Watch when you are vulnerable because with the Unusual No-Trump you will ask your partner to bid at the three level and if partner only has two of either of your long suits 5/5 that may not be enough.

One last thing about responding to your partner's Michaels Cue bid. Your LHO has opened 1h and your partner bids 2h and your RHO passes. Your partner is telling you that she holds at least five Spades and an unspecified minor – but which minor? If you are interested to find out which minor just bid 2nt and your partner will tell you by bidding the minor.

Modified Pottage – I've called it Modified Pottage for a long time now and for the life of me I cannot remember why and I am not that sure the name is correct. Modified Pottage to me it is and the way I play this convention is as follows:

It is a defence to 1nt.   The opposition open 1nt (weak no-trump) and I have length in a major or in a minor and I will bid 2c or 2d asking my partner to bid a suit. A bid of:

2c will ask partner to bid best minor suit
or
2d will ask partner to bid best major suit

and that's about it. I will be holding near or opening points and 5/5 cards in the minor suits or 5/5 in the major suits and I am simply asking partner to bid the best suit.

If your partner bids 2c or 2d after opposition opening bid of 1nt and no response from opener's partner, then do as your partner asks. Bid your best suit. 2c will ask for best minor and if the Club suit is your best minor then just pass and if you have extra values then jump. If your partner bids 2c and your best suit is Diamonds then simply bid 2d. The same if your partner bids 2d asking you to bid your best major.

Sharples

There is the official version and the version I see at the various clubs which is the popular version and dead easy. It is an alternative to the Modified Pottage convention described earlier. If you are interested in your partner's best suit after opponent's 1nt opening bid then all you do is bid 2c and your partner will oblige and bid best suit at the next available level if weak but with eight or less losing tricks in hand then partner will show that by a jump. If weak and Clubs is the best suit then partner will pass.

Landy

After opposition 1nt, bid 2c which says *'partner – I've both the majors split 5/5 so would you bid your best major.'*

Those are the three popular 1nt defence bids. Obviously if you use the 2c bid as a defence to opponent's 1nt to enquire about partner's hand, you will of course have to decide which of the three conventions you and your partner are going to use. You can only use one of them. The advantages of using this defence to 1nt is:

- it will stop the partner of the 1nt opener, bidding 2c for Stayman and thus may hinder them finding a four card major.
- if you find a fit and win the contract then you do know where 12-14 points are sitting.

I have an arrangement with one of my regular partners. If my partner bids 1nt and the opposition bid a conventional 2c defence bid which stops me from bidding 2c Stayman, I simply Double which tells my partner that I would have bid 2c had it not been for the interference by the opposition.

I'm all for upsetting the opposition plans but in a pleasant and friendly manner but if you use either of these three conventions, remember to satisfy yourself that the opposition's 1nt opening bid is a 12-14 pointer and not a strong no-trump opening.

Using a defence to 1nt is not all plain sailing.

There will be occasions when you will be frustrated and not be able to call 2c or 2d after the opposition 1nt bid, having extra length in Clubs or Diamonds because your partner will rightly construe your bid as a defence to 1nt and will respond accordingly. So frustrating when at the club you find that a 2c or 2d bid has been successful and you were unable to make the bid because of the agreed defence to no- trump convention.

The Splinter Bid. Is a seemingly unnecessary jump bid. The bid guarantees support for partner's opening bid suit but also shows in addition, a singleton or void in the suit in which the jump is made which is the Splinter bid and invites slam.   For example look at this illustration.

Your partner, the opener, bids 1h. Holding this hand you could respond by jumping straight to 4h but using the Splinter convention you respond - stop 4d hence the description of being a seemingly

♠	K842
♥	AJ73
♦	7
♣	AQ94

unnecessary bid. The bid guarantees four card support of the Hearts and also a singleton or a void in Diamonds – the Splinter bid suit. Your partner then knows about the support and the singleton or void and can make the decision as to 4h or exploring the possibility of a slam.

I was going to describe the **Multi 2 Diamond** Opening bid but I will leave that for another day. If, when at your local Bridge club you come across this bid by the opposition, simply ask the partner of the person who makes the bid what the bid means and you will probably get an unsatisfactory answer which could prompt another question resulting in yet another unsatisfactory answer. If you are like me, you will then probably be none the wiser. The Multi 2 Diamond bid is an opening of 2d which is alertable. The bid is designed to make it difficult for the opponents and it often stops them finding out straight away which major is intended. The major suit is unknown as is the strength of the opener.

Friendly game – Bridge.

Benjamin Acol

A very popular convention. You will come across many partnerships at Bridge clubs who use the convention commonly called Benji. Basically, the Benjamin convention shows a strong hand when opening at the 2 level in a minor but a weak hand when opening at the 2 level in a major.

In practice there seems to be several slight variations of Mr Albert Benjamin's convention and the one variation which I believe is quite popular and one that I use is as follows:

Opening	What it means
2c	A strong opening promising 21-22 points or 8 playing tricks in any suit
2d	A strong opening promising 23 plus points. This is the same as the strong 2c bid when not using Benjamin.
2h	Shows a six card Heart suit with 5 – 10 points in hand. 5/9 points when not vulnerable and 6/10 points otherwise.
2s	Shows a six card Spade suit with 5 – 10 points in hand. 5/9 points when not vulnerable and 6/10 points otherwise.
2nt	Shows balanced hand and 19/20 points.

The Basics of the 'Benji' – Benjamin Acol system I use.

It is a pre-emptive system allowing an opening in a Major at the two level with less than an Acol opening hand. It presumes a six card suit with points between 5 and 10. If not vulnerable then play at 5/9 points but when vulnerable best to have between 6 and 10 points.

Why use the 'Benji' Convention?
- As a pre-emptive bid as it cuts out bidding space for the opposition.
- If your partner has a good hand it provides the basis for reaching game which might not otherwise be found.
- It provides information to your partner on which a sacrifice bid may be made (usually of non vul. playing against a vul. pair). For example you open 2s with say 8 points and your partner holds only 6/7 points but with 4 cards in the Spade suit. The opposition with 25/26 points reach a Heart contract and your partner can now sacrifice in four Spades prepared to go 3 down doubled for a score of 500 when not vulnerable and stopping the opponents making 4 Hearts vulnerable and scoring 620.

Responding to a 'Benji' 2 opening in a major. – 2h or 2s.

- With less than an opening hand, pass unless you have good cards in the opening suit and you want to be competitive and push the opposition up. This can have a negative effect as you may push them into game, which they might not otherwise reach.

- With a good opening hand and support for the suit, bid 2nt. This is a conventional bid, which should be alerted, and is nothing to do with playing in no-trumps. It is saying *'partner' we may have game on in your suit. Please explain your hand further.*

225

- After a 2 opening in a major, partner's response in another suit must show a severe shortage in your suit and at least six cards in another suit. For example, after a 2h opening, 2s should show no help in Hearts, having a void or a small singleton – and 6+ Spade holding. After a 2h opening your bid of 3c or 3d will show a pre-emptive 7 card suit again with no help in Hearts.

Again judgement comes into play. If your partner opens 2h or 2s and you hold less than 10 points you know for a fact that your combined count is 15+ and the opposition may have game on. Watch the vulnerability; it often pays to pass and let them get on with it.

<u>Opener's Rebid</u> – Unless your partner responds 2nt asking you to describe your hand, you will seldom have a rebid.

So you've opened 2h or 2s and your partner bids 2nt asking you to describe your hand which you will do a follows:

- A rebid of 3c shows minimum points of 5/6.

- A rebid of 3d shows 7/8 points mostly in opening suit.

- A rebid of 3h shows 7/8 points mostly in outside suits.

- A rebid of 3s shows 9/10 points. Max. for your opening bid.

- A rebid of 3nt shows specifically AKQ of your opening suit.

You then leave it to your partner to decide at which level you are to play. Your partner knows your strength and has to make a judgement. Even if the opposition came in with a sacrifice bid it is your partner who is most likely to be best placed to decide whether to double or to bid at the five level.

<u>Opening 2c and 2d when playing 'Benji'</u>. Because an opening of 2 in a major shows a weak hand, there has to be a conventional opening to show a strong hand.

- An opening 2c shows either a balanced 21/22 points or 8 playing tricks in any suit. Many folk play a compulsory 2d bid as a relay for opener to then describe hand. Others play 2d as a negative (less than 7 points). After opener rebids 2nt showing 21/22 points, Stayman can be used to find a 4/4 major fit.

- An opening of 2d is equal to the Acol 2c opening

After all that here's a summary of 'Benji'
Open 2h or 2s showing between 5 and 10 points and a six card suit. Your partner will less than an opening hand will pass unless good card are held in partner's suit. With opening hand, partner will support and respond 2nt asking opener to explain hand further.

- 3c – shows minimum points 5/6
- 3d – shows 7/8 points in opening suit.
- 3h - shows 7/8 points in outside suits.
- 3s – shows 9/10 points
- 3nt – shows specifically AKQ of opening suit.

Opening 2c shows either a balanced 21/22 points in which case the rebid is 2nt or 8 playing tricks in any suit in which case the rebid is that suit. Responding to 2c opening is compulsory 2d as a relay for opener to then describe hand. After opener rebids 2nt then Stayman can be used. Opening 2d is the same as the Acol 2c strong opening 2c bid.

Now to finish have a go at the following quiz and see how much you have taken on board. So as not to mark the pages of this book put your answers on a separate sheet of paper and check them with my answers which are at the end of the quiz.

Part 1 – All to do with Numbers – 20 questions

1	After your 1nt opening, your partner bids 2nt. – Transfers not agreed. What points are being confirmed?	
2	Your partner has supported your opening 1 level suit bid at the 2 level. The minimum number of points in your partner's hand?	
3	Your partner opened 1d and you responded 1s. Your partner then rebids – stop 2nt. What point range is being confirmed?	
4	What is the point range of a weak 1nt opening?	
5	Your partner has responded 1nt to your opening bid of 1h. What is your partner's point range?	
6	Your partner has overcalled 1nt to the opposition bid of 1d. Your partner will have cover in the Diamonds bid by the opposition but what range of points?	
7	Transfers have been agreed. You open 1nt and your partner bids 2nt. How many points in partner's hand?	
8	Your partner opened the bidding 1d and you responded 1h and then your partner rebid 1nt after which you bid 2nt. Exactly how many points will you have in your hand?	
9	You opened 1nt and your partner responds 2h. What is the maximum number of points your partner will have in hand for the weak take-out?	
10	You open the bidding stop 3c. What is your point range?	

11	You open the bidding 1h and your partner responds 2c. You then rebid 2nt. What will be your range of points?	
12	You open the bidding stop 2nt. What is your point range?	
13	How many points would you normally be showing if you opened the bidding stop 2c?	
14	The gentleman on your right opens 1nt. You then overcall 2h. What is the minimum number of points your partner expects you to have?	
15	The lady on your right opens 1h and you overcall 2d. What is your range of points?	
16	You respond 2d to your partner's opening 2c bid. What maximum number of points in hand?	
17	You respond 2c to partner's 1nt bid. You will normally have not less than ? points.	
18	Your partner has doubled the opposition 1nt bid. What range of points in partner's hand?	
19	Your partner bids 1s after you have doubled the opening bid of 1d. What is the minimum number of points your partner will have in hand?	
20	Your response to your partner's opening 1h bid is 1nt. What range of points in your hand?	

Part 2 – All to do with responding to your partner's opening bid.

You may find it easier to set out the hands before you.

A	Your hand		Your partner opens	What would you bid? Stayman agreed but not Transfers.
♠	8632		1nt	
♥	K6		1d	
♦	AJ432		1h	
♣	83		1s	

B	Your hand		Your partner opens	What would you bid? Stayman and Transfers agreed
♠	98632		1nt	
♥	Q6		1d	
♦	Q432		1c	
♣	86		1s	

C	Your hand		Your partner opens	What would you bid? Stayman and Transfers agreed
♠	AJ83		1nt	
♥	8643		1c	
♦	KQ3		1s	
♣	Q2		1h	

Part 2 – continued.

D	Your hand		Your partner opens	What would you bid? Stayman agreed but not transfers.
♠	A83		2nt	
♥	K94		1d	
♦	97642		1h	
♣	96		2c	

E	Your hand		Your partner opens	What would you bid? Stayman and Transfers agreed
♠	92		1nt	
♥	AK8		1d	
♦	KJ74		1h	
♣	K843		1s	

F	Your hand		Your partner opens	What would you bid? Stayman and Transfers agreed
♠	K9		1nt	
♥	AJ82		1c	
♦	K974		1h	
♣	Q843		1d	

Part 3 –

All to do with your rebid
after your partner has responded.
You may find it easier to set out the hands before you.

1 - Holding this hand you opened 1nt. Stayman agreed but not Transfers. What is your rebid if your partner responded?

♠	AK43
♥	J632
♦	K6
♣	QJ4

a. 2s -

b. 2c -

c. 2nt -

2 - Holding this hand you opened 1h. What is your rebid if your partner responded?

♠	AQ43
♥	J854
♦	K32
♣	AK8

a. 1nt -

b. 2h -

c. 1s -

3 - Holding this hand you opened 1nt. Stayman and Transfers agreed. What is your rebid if your partner responded?

♠	K76
♥	Q76
♦	QJ84
♣	A85

a. 2nt -

b. 2c -

c. 2d -

Part 3 continued

4 - Holding this hand you opened 1d. What is your rebid if your partner responded?

♠	9
♥	AQ53
♦	AQ763
♣	KQ5

a. 1s -

b. 2c -

c. 1h -

5 - Holding this hand you opened 1d. What is your rebid if your partner responded?

♠	A75
♥	K4
♦	AQ54
♣	AQ74

a. 1h -

b. 1nt -

c. 2c -

Part 4 – All to do with your partner's rebid, if any, after you have rebid following your partner's response to your opening bid.

You may find it easier to set out the hands before you.

1 Opener	Opener bids 1s	Responder
♠ A854	Responder replies 2c.	♠ K76
♥ K65	Opener rebids 2nt.	♥ Q98
♦ QJ98		♦ 43
♣ AJ	Responder's bid ?	♣ K9864

2 Opener	1h by opener.	Responder
♠ K3	1s response.	♠ A986
♥ Q9752	2d rebid by opener.	♥ AK5
♦ AK32		♦ 76
♣ 85	Responder's rebid?	♣ J762

3 Opener	Opener bids 1s	Responder
♠ Q9542	Responder bids 2c	♠ KJ7
♥ AQ9	Opener rebids 2d	♥ K76
♦ K9543		♦ J7
♣ Void	Responder's rebid ?	♣ A8754

4 Opener	Opener begins with 1h	Responder
♠ Q	Responder bids 2c	♠ A987
♥ KQJ53	Opener rebids 3d	♥ 8
♦ K986		♦ Q5
♣ KQ3	Responder's rebid?	♣ A98742

5 Opener	Opening bid 1h.	Responder
♠ 3	Responder bids 1s,	♠ AK542
♥ K9752	Opener rebids 2d	♥ A
♦ AQ86		♦ 9542
♣ KJ8	Responder's rebid?	♣ Q43

Part 5 –

The opener is left to make the final decision.

You may find it easier to set out the hands before you.

A	Opener	1nt opening bid.		Responder
♠	K985	2c Stayman response.	♠	AJ74
♥	AQ76	Opener replies 2h	♥	K86
♦	Q97	Responder's rebid – stop 3nt	♦	KJ6
♣	K9	What does Opener bid?	♣	J86

B	Opener	Opener bids 1nt.		Responder
♠	KJ98	Responder bids Stayman 2c	♠	A76
♥	QJ4	Opener replies 2s.	♥	A854
♦	Q54	Responder rebids 2nt.	♦	J874
♣	KJ3	What does Opener bid?	♣	Q8

C	Opener	1h from opener.		Responder
♠	QJ7	Responder bids 1s	♠	K985
♥	K943	Opener rebids 1nt – Reverse	♥	A63
♦	AJ98	Responder rebids 2nt.	♦	1064
♣	KJ	What does Opener bid?	♣	Q98

D	Opener	1h from opener.		Responder
♠	5	2h response.	♠	J96
♥	KQJ865		♥	9742
♦	AKJ2		♦	73
♣	97	Opener's bullish rebid?	♣	KQ82

Part 6 - Some Odds and Some S.........undries.

1. Your partner has opened the bidding stop 2c and you have a Yarborough.   What do you bid?

2. Your partner has opened 1nt and your right hand opposition doubles.   What do you do if you hold less than seven points?

3. Your partner doubles an opening bid of 1h and your right hand opponent passes.   What is expected of you?

4. You have agreed Transfers and your partner responds 2d to your 1nt opening. What is your partner asking you to bid?

5. You've reached the stage of bidding when you ask your partner to tell you the number of Aces in hand and you bid Gerber 4c. Your partner then bids 4h.
   How many Aces are being confirmed?

6. You have reached the stage of bidding when you ask your partner to tell you the number of Aces in hand and you bid Blackwood 4nt. Your partner replies 5c.
   How many Aces does your partner hold?

7. You hold the following hand and partner has not bid.
   What card would you lead against a:

♠	9
♥	Q943
♦	AQJ93
♣	983

3nt contract.

3h contract.

4s contract

8. You are not vulnerable and you have achieved your 3nt contract
   with one trick over.　　　What is your score?

9. Your partner has opened 1h and you hold this hand.
   What would you bid?

♠	KJ93
♥	943
♦	Q952
♣	K8

a. if the opposition overcalled 1s.

b. if the opposition pass.

10. What would you bid holding the hand?

♠	Q93
♥	43
♦	A972
♣	QJ94

Your partner has overcalled 1s and the opener's
partner has supported and bid 2h.

Part 7 –

You are dealer.
What would you bid holding these 10 hands?

1
- ♠ AK94
- ♥ J8752
- ♦ A94
- ♣ Void

2
- ♠ A6
- ♥ K85
- ♦ QJ652
- ♣ K63

3
- ♠ J972
- ♥ AKQ3
- ♦ K843
- ♣ 4

4
- ♠ AJ84
- ♥ KQ2
- ♦ AK8
- ♣ KJ3

5
- ♠ J986532
- ♥ K2
- ♦ 984
- ♣ Q

6
- ♠ Void
- ♥ K8643
- ♦ AKQ76
- ♣ 843

7
- ♠ AKJ4
- ♥ KQ7
- ♦ AK
- ♣ QJ43

8
- ♠ K96542
- ♥ A
- ♦ 9763
- ♣ K92

9
- ♠ K87
- ♥ QJ
- ♦ A84
- ♣ Q9764

10
- ♠ void
- ♥ AJ984
- ♦ K8742
- ♣ Q64

Answers to The Bridge Quiz

Part 1

1	11/12	5	6/10	9	10	13	23 or more	17	11
2	6	6	15/18	10	5-9	14	10	18	15/18
3	17/18	7	12	11	15/16	15	10/15	19	0
4	12/14	8	9	12	20/22	16	7	20	6/10

Part 2

A
2d – A weak take-out
1s – Never deny 4
   card major
1s – Never deny 4
   card major
Stop 3s – 8 losers.

B
2h – transfer
Pass – less than
   6 points.
Pass – less than
   6 points
Pass – less than
   6 points.

C
2c – Stayman
1h – bid up the line

Stop 3s – losing
   trick count
Stop 3h – losing
   trick count

D
3nt
2d – supporting

1nt – cannot bid 2d
   only 7 points
3d – with A & K

E
3nt
2c – see what
   partner rebids
2c – see what
   partner rebids
Stop 3nt

F
2c - Stayman
1h – see what
   partner rebids
3h or 4h

1h – see what
   partner rebids

Part 3

1
Pass - weak
   take-out
2h - reply to
   Stayman
3nt – with max
   points

2
2n t- inviting
   game
3h – inviting
   game
3s – inviting
   game

3
Pass – game
   chance ?
2d – neg.
   Stayman
2h – transfer

4
2nt- reversing
   17/18pts
2h - jumping
   fence
3h - inviting
   game

5
3nt – 19
   points
3nt – game
   points
3nt – game
   points

A Relaxed Refresher in the Art of Bridge

Part 4

1	**Responder's passes** – knowing that partner has only 15/16 pts and was forced to bid 2nt because of the 2c bid. If opener had had more points then opener would have bid 3nt knowing that responder had at least 8 points to bid 2c
2	**Responder bids 4h.** Knowing that partner has at least 12pts & 5 hearts having bid another suit at the 2 level, in spite of only 12 points, holding 3 hearts including the AK is confident to bid stop 4h.
3	**Responder bids 3s.** After opening 1s and a rebid of 2d, responder knows that partner has 5 Spades. Holding 12 points and three Spades making the fit, responder will invite game confirming the lack of game points.
4	**Responder bids 3nt.** Responder has not failed to notice that partner's rebid of Diamonds was a fence jump and thus holding 16 or so points. With 10 points in hand and the unbid suit covered the responder bids to game – 3nt.
5	**Responder bids 3c.** Knowing that the Hearts and Diamonds and Spades are covered, the responder wishes to know whether the Clubs are safe in order to achieve a no-trump contract. Responder bids the fourth suit having half a stop – a conventional bid, which asks partner to bid no-trumps if the suit is stopped in hand. Opener would bid to game – 3nt.

Part 5

A	**Opener bids 4s.** Responder has asked for a four card major and did nothing about the Heart reply. Responder must have game points in hand to bid 3nt plus at least four spades. Opener has 4 Spades as well.
B	**Opener should pass.** A poor 13 point hand and partner has only 11/12 points.
C	**Opener should pass.** Responder would have passed with less than 9 points and bid to game with more than 9 points so responder must have exactly 9 points. No point in bidding to game with only 15/16 in hand.
D	**Opener should bid to game – 4h.** Normally when holding a weak opening hand and partner supports at the next level you would consider one up-shut up but the distribution here dictates otherwise. The responder has at least 6 points opposite and those 6 point might even include the Ace of Hearts.

Part 6.

1	Bid 2d - confirming 7 or less points.	6	None or 4
2	Bid your longest suit as a take-out.	7	Q♦ 9♠ 3♥
3	Bid best suit – if less than 8 losers then jump.	8	430
4	2h	9	You bid 1nt You bid 1s
5	1 Ace.	10	2s – you know your partner has at least five Spades.

Part 7

1	2	3	4	5	6	7	8	9	10
1h	1nt	1h	2nt	pass	1h	2c	1s	1nt	1h

240

A final few words

As I said right at the beginning, this book is intended for those who play Bridge and who feel their game would be better if they brushed up on one or two things.

"If only I knew you had the master Diamond I would have led Diamonds and then we would have defeated the contract." The partnership could have agreed one of the several discard systems.

"It would have been much better had my weak hand gone on the table as the Dummy rather than your stronger hand." This could have been resolved had the partnership agreed to Transfers.

"We got too high up in the bidding to find we were short of two Aces." Using Gerber may have helped or even a cue bid.

"How was I to know your opening hand was as strong as that?"
The opener's rebid would have shown a strong or weak hand.

"I'm not going to open at the three level again."
A significant casualty was probably because the rules of opening at the three level were not observed.

I do hope you have found the book helpful
and that your game improves as a result.

Have fun with your Bridge.

Bryan left school at 16 and started with a bank and twenty or so years later he joined one his customers who specialised in the sale of private residential care and nursing homes, to set up and head a department which raised funds for care home purchasers. He retired in the early 90's and through one of his Mother's friends was introduced to Bridge.

After moving to the English Sussex coast and joining three local bridge clubs, several of Bryan's new neighbours wanted to learn the game and from there Bryan's first book *The Road Across the Bridge* was written. Bryan has been married to Margaret for 46 years and has a son John and daughter Mandy plus three grand-children, Yasmin, Jad and Lucia.

Bryan now considers his wife Margaret has actually 'turned the corner' because some of her bidding and play does now start to make a little sense which Bryan considers a bit scary to say the least. Bryan's ambition now is to persuade Margaret to join him at the local Bridge club one evening and time will tell whether or not he is successful.

ISBN 142515698-3